marie claire

food fast

thank you

Catie Ziller, my publisher, for her support, faith and trust. Petrina Tinslay for sharing her talent, patience and total commitment to perfection with me. Vanessa "welcome to my world" Holden—I am very glad you did. Your design talents have taken the book further and thank you for your dedication to having things "just so". Matt Handbury and Murdoch Magazines for their continual strong support of food. To Paula Berge, thank you for keeping my sense of humour going, the props coming in and out, the business operating and basically life running. Ben Masters and Briget Palmer—my backbone, recipe testers and photography chefs—thanks for the long haul and your endless enthusiasm. Tony Lee and Smeg Appliances for supplying the total wish list and amazing kitchen for the studio. Shelly and Joy at Mud Australia for indulging me with my own colour of their amazing ceramics in perfect shapes and drop-dead wonderful matt glaze. Dee Bates, simply the perfect PR personified. Susin Chow for your encouragement along the long road of being editor. Thank you for making sense of all those words. Jody Vassallo, thank you for always being there.

Starting with perfect produce helps—a big thank you to everyone at Antico's, Demcos, Paddington Fresh Foods and Mohr Foods; Country Road for their clothes and homewares; Malcolm Greenwood, Global Knives and Dinosaur Designs for the wonderful props.

Thank you Michael Bell, Pinnacle Stainless Steel, Paul Thomas, Jimmy O, Chris and Simon Andrews for building me a studio and kitchen yesterday. My partner Billy for your energy, support, love and building skills—thank you. Thank you to my family.

Published in 1999 by Merehurst Limited, Ferry House, 51–57 Lacy Road, Putney, London SW15 1PR.

Art Director/Designer: Vanessa Holden
Author and Stylist: Donna Hay
Photographer: Petrina Tinslay
Editor: Susin Chow
CEO and Publisher: Anne Wilson; Associate Publisher: Catie Ziller; International Sales Director: Mark Newman; Marketing and Sales Manager: Kathryn Harvey

Cover: Warmed olive and garlic pasta (page 72) served with sesame sweet potato (page 134).

A catalogue record for this book is available from the British Library.
ISBN 1-85391-857-1

Text © Donna Hay 1999. Photography © Petrina Tinslay 1999. Design © Murdoch Books® 1999. Printed by Toppan Printing Hong Kong Co. Ltd. PRINTED IN CHINA. First printed 1999.

Distributed in the UK by D Services, 6 Euston Street, Freeman's Common, Leicester LE2 7SS, Telephone (0116) 254 7671, Facsimile (0116) 254 4670.

First published in Australia by Murdoch Books® , 45 Jones Street, Ultimo NSW 2007, Australia.

marie claire

food fast

donna hay

photography by
petrina tinslay

MEREHURST

contents

introduction

Time. Today, it makes sense to make clever use of the little bit you have.

marie claire food fast offers stylish and innovative meal-time solutions for busy people—for a fast solo dinner on the couch or a casual catch-up with friends. From the familiar to the formal, it is full of clever ideas that start at breakfast and take you right through to dinner (and beyond).

Quick-fix classics like pasta are given a modern twist, joined by simple but satisfying flavour combinations, put together with a minimum of fuss. We show you the keys to keeping a well-stocked pantry, catching current produce and utilising straight-forward cooking techniques for no-fuss food in a matter of minutes.

To complement this simple, fresh approach, a comprehensive basics chapter is included, as well as a chapter of quick short top and sides for a range of fresh and delicious menu options. More information about ingredients and cooking terms marked with a star* can be found in the glossary.

in the kit chen

shop

Shopping is easier if you have a rough list. Try breaking your shopping into sections to make it quicker and more organised.

staple shop

Make a list so you don't arrive home without things you need. Go through your pantry or try to remember what you have cooked over the previous days so you can restock the staples such as rice, pasta and flour. Shop for meat and chicken up to three days in advance as long as you store it correctly. Purchase fresh vegetables three days in advance. (See store, page 12.)

quick shop

Why not use the Internet to do some of your shopping. Some supermarkets have listings of every product from their shelves for you to choose from a web site. These often include paying by credit card over the Net and delivery —how civil. If you are busy at work all day and you need to do a fast shop on the way home, why not try to place a fax or phone order to your regular butcher, fruit and vegetable providore, fishmonger etc, for a speedy pick-up.

special shop

I like to venture out to the core of ethnic food stores where I can find the best of my speciality shopping. Once every 2–3 months, I stock up on Asian groceries, Italian deli items and pastas, Mediterranean spices, breads and preserves and all those great ingredients the world has to offer.

get fresh

When shopping, buying the freshest and best quality available is important. If you start with good, fresh ingredients then you are more than halfway there. Follow these tips so you can purchase the best quality.

When buying meat, the surface of cut meat such as steaks should be moist and a full deep red colour. The fat should be either a good creamy white colour or a creamy yellow colour which usually comes from grain-fed beef. The fat should also be supple and moist.

Chicken should be plump and firm-looking, not tired and flat. The skin should be moist and will vary from white to yellow for corn-fed chickens. When buying chicken pieces, make sure that they are moist but not sitting in any water or liquid. The flesh should have a pinkish tinge which turns to a green hue when the chicken is spoilt.

Seafood is easy to identify as fresh when you are buying it. All seafood should have a pleasant sea smell. Whole fish should have a clear eye, not clouded. Oysters should be in a cold fridge or packed between ice. The oyster should look plump and moist. Prawns and crustaceans in general should have no discolouration around the legs and a firm intact shell. Do not buy seafood that is sitting in water or in melted ice as the flavour and texture of the seafood will have deteriorated.

Cheese is best purchased from a speciality cheese shop where they should have more knowledge about the cheese, its ripeness and its flavour. Remember when purchasing cheese to have an idea of when you will be serving and eating the cheese. Buy a runny soft ripe Brie for tonight and a Brie with a thin chalky core through it for 4–6 days time.

store

If you have a well-stocked pantry, fridge and freezer then cooking a fast and fresh meal should be a breeze.

pantry

Make sure that your pantry is cool, dark, well-ventilated, and not musty or damp. Organised shelves make it easy to see what ingredients you have and are therefore faster to cook. It is a good idea to group ingredients together, such as Asian sauces, rices, pasta, condiments and spices, as you will find the ingredients quickly and it is also easier to prepare a shopping list when foods are grouped.

The pantry is the place where you can store all those items, ready for a quick meal or when friends drop by for a drink and a bite to eat. Cornichons and crackers or oatcakes to serve with cheese and pâté are a great starting point.

snap freeze

Purchased frozen products should be returned to the freezer as soon as possible. If you are freezing foods such as stocks or homemade ice cream, make sure that it is covered well and placed in the coldest part of the freezer with enough clear space around it so the cold air can freeze the food quickly and evenly. The food should be covered tightly to exclude air and to prevent freezer burn which dries the food and makes it very tough. If you wish to chill or freeze food very quickly then use a metal container and cover.

perishables

Meat and chicken will last up to three days in the fridge if removed from the plastic bag and placed on a plate. Cover with aluminium foil or loosely with plastic wrap. Store in the coldest part of the fridge (usually at the back) away from the fridge fan to prevent drying. Fish is best purchased on the day or one day before using because the taste of fresh fish is always best. Place gutted and scaled fish in an airtight container or tightly wrapped in plastic.

I prefer to purchase my vegetables fresh every two or, at the most, three days. Store leafy vegetables wrapped in damp tea towels in the crisper or on the lower shelves of the fridge. Mushrooms should be stored in paper bags so that they can breathe—even the ones you can purchase in plastic trays should be stored in paper or muslin bags. Potatoes should be stored in a cool dark place such as in the bottom of a well-ventilated pantry. Herbs in bunches have a longer life if you snip the stems and place them in a jug of water. Cover them with a damp tea towel or a plastic bag and then store them in the refrigerator.

Cheese and cured meats often come in plastic. If the wrapping is airtight, there is no need to remove the plastic. Cheese is best stored in a cheesecloth or calico (cotton) bag to prevent it from sweating. Cured meats such as prosciutto should be stored in the deli paper you purchased it in or loosely wrapped in plastic wrap.

Dairy items such as milk should be stored on the fridge shelves and not in the door as most would expect. Because the door is often opened, it is said to be the warmest and most fluctuating part of the fridge. My milk seems to be fine in the door of the fridge and it fits nicely and it looks like it belongs there, but my fridge also has a good fan in it which circulates the cold air and I think most modern fridges do, too.

prep

Get organised and get a head start on the task at hand. You'll cut your cooking time and stress levels when time is of the essence.

prepare to cook

Fill your pantry with basic and convenient stores to save on prep time and get you cooking faster. Start with flour: plain, self-raising and rice. Sugar in variations from the basic white, caster (superfine) and brown to demerera and palm. Rices such as arborio for risotto, jasmine, long and short grain. A variety of pastas of different thickness and weight to hold different sauces. Couscous, quick-cooking polenta and lentils are also pantry assets. Olive, sesame, vegetable and chilli oils are a must. A few vinegars like white and red wine, balsamic and cider will also be handy. Quality cooking wine has a better flavour through the food so have a bottle of red, dry white and dessert wine on hand.

Convenient stores include quality bottled tomato pasta sauce, curry and laksa pastes, canned Italian plum tomatoes, quality canned tuna in oil, canned beans, anchovies in salt or oil, marinated olives, salted capers and liquid stock.

Fill the refrigerator with a few cheeses including parmesan, cheddar and maybe a blue or ricotta, and dairy items such as milk, yoghurt, butter and cream. Many condiments and sauces need to be refrigerated after opening. Great flavour bases or boosters to a meal include condiments such as mustards, horseradish, chutneys, Asian chilli paste, miso paste and wasabi paste, and sauces such oyster, soy, hoisin, sweet chilli, and fish.

get busy

When returning from shopping and before storing, trim steaks of any fat or sinew, trim and prepare chicken, and clean, rinse and pat dry seafood. Trim and chop vegetables and greens, cover them well and store in the fridge until required. To revive salad greens before serving, place in bowls of cold water with a few cubes of ice to refresh.

Shred ginger, chop chillies and garlic or slice onions and store in separate little bowls covered tightly with plastic wrap in the fridge. Freeze lemon or lime juice in ice cube containers to save time and effort later.

Foods to be marinated can be prepared ahead of time, as long as you are not marinating meat, chicken or fish in lots of acid, like vinegar or lemon juice, for more than 2–3 hours. The acid will breakdown the texture of meat.

Remove foods such as cheese, chocolate and rich chocolate cakes from the refrigerator so that they have plenty of time to return to room temperature and will have regained their full flavour when served.

time wise

There are some things that definitely need to be cooked just before serving time. If serving hot, cook meat, chicken or seafood just before serving—reheating is drying and nasty.

Chop herbs such as parsley, chervil, mint and basil so that they have a fresh full flavour and are not discoloured. Always dress a leaf salad last as the dressing often makes the leaves soggy if allowed to stand for any amount of time.

food fast

10 minutes (or so)

panini

couscous

noodles

wraps

egg rolls

pasta

melts

steamed greens

lemongrass broth

sashimi

egg rolls

pasta with fresh tomato and rocket sauce

mussels in ginger and lemongrass broth

egg rolls

2 teaspoons sesame oil
4 shallots (green onions), chopped
4 eggs
fillings such as smoked salmon, smoked chicken, rocket
(arugula), baby English spinach, chopped tomato
thick sweet soy sauce to serve

Heat sesame oil in a large, nonstick frying pan over medium
heat. Add the shallots and cook for 2 minutes. Remove half
the shallots and set aside.
Beat eggs lightly to combine them. Add half the egg to the
pan and swirl the pan to evenly coat the base. Cook for
2–3 minutes or until almost set. Slide the egg from the pan
and place fillings of your choice down one side of the egg.
Roll up and serve with thick soy. Repeat with remaining
ingredients. Serves 2.

pasta with fresh tomato and rocket sauce

400g (13 oz) fresh pasta*
5 very ripe Roma or ox-heart tomatoes*, finely chopped
2 teaspoons salted capers, rinsed
1/4 red onion, finely chopped
2 tablespoons olive oil
3 tablespoons shredded basil
2 cups roughly chopped rocket (arugula)
200g (61/2 oz) fresh ricotta
cracked black pepper

Place pasta into a saucepan of boiling water, cook
for 4–5 minutes or until al dente, and drain.
Combine tomatoes, capers, onion, oil, basil, rocket, ricotta
and pepper. Toss through the hot pasta and finish with
parmesan cheese. Serves 4.

mussels in ginger and lemongrass broth

3 cups (24 fl oz) fish stock
2 tablespoons shredded ginger
2 stalks lemongrass*, finely chopped
2 teaspoons shredded lemon rind
1kg (2 lb) mussels, cleaned

Place stock, ginger, lemongrass and lemon rind in a
saucepan over high heat. Bring the broth to the boil then
add the mussels and cook for 2–3 minutes or until the
mussels have opened. Discard any mussels that don't
open. Serve mussels in deep bowls with the broth and
some bread. Serves 4.

sashimi on gingered noodle salad

tuna sashimi* for 4 people
soy and wasabi* to serve
gingered noodle salad
250g (8 oz) dry cellophane (beanthread) noodles*
1/3 cup pickled ginger
2 cups small watercress sprigs
3 tablespoons roughly chopped coriander
3 tablespoons soy sauce
2 tablespoons sesame seeds

To make the gingered noodle salad, place the cellophane
noodles into a bowl of boiling water and soak them for
2 minutes; drain.
Toss the noodles with the ginger, watercress, coriander,
soy and sesame.
Place the noodle salad on serving plates and top with slices
of tuna sashimi. Serve with extra soy and wasabi. Serves 4.

lamb cutlets with chilli noodles

8–12 lamb cutlets
oil
cracked black pepper
chilli noodles
1 tablespoon sesame oil
1 tablespoon chilli oil*
3 red chillies, seeded and chopped
2 tablespoons shredded ginger
2 cloves garlic, sliced
3 tablespoons basil, or Thai basil leaves*
500g (1 lb) fresh rice noodles, rinsed under hot water
soy sauce to serve

Brush the cutlets with oil and sprinkle with pepper. Cook
under a hot preheated grill or in a hot frying pan for
1–2 minutes on each side or until cooked to your liking.
While cutlets are cooking, heat sesame and chilli oils in a
wok or frying pan over high heat. Add chillies, ginger, garlic
and basil and cook for 1 minute. Add the noodles and cook
for 3–4 minutes or until heated through. Serve the noodles
with the lamb cutlets and small bowls of soy sauce on
the side. Serves 4.

sashimi on gingered noodle salad

lamb cutlets with chilli noodles

pasta with smoked salmon and dill sauce

asparagus with tofu and balsamic butter

squid with green chilli and kaffir lime

pasta with smoked salmon and dill sauce

500g (1 lb) fresh fettucine or linguini*
4 tablespoons olive oil
2 tablespoons lemon juice
1 tablespoon salted capers, rinsed
1 tablespoon wholegrain mustard
1/2 red onion, finely sliced
8–10 slices smoked salmon
2 tablespoons chopped dill
2 tablespoons chopped flat-leaf (Italian) parsley

Place pasta in a large saucepan of boiling water over high heat and cook for 5 minutes or until al dente. While pasta is cooking, place oil, lemon juice, capers, mustard and onion in a small saucepan over low-medium heat and cook for 2 minutes or until heated through. Drain pasta and place in a large serving bowl. Toss through the oil and lemon mixture, salmon, dill and parsley. Serve with lots of cracked black pepper and a salad of baby English spinach. Serves 4.

asparagus with tofu and balsamic butter

1 tablespoon oil
2 cloves garlic, sliced
60g (2 oz) butter
3 tablespoons balsamic vinegar
3 tablespoons water
1 bunch asparagus, trimmed and halved
cracked black pepper
4 thick slices firm silken tofu
1 tablespoon thyme sprigs

Heat oil in a frying pan over medium heat. Add garlic and cook for 1 minute. Add butter, balsamic and water to the pan and cook for 1 minute.
Add the asparagus and pepper to the pan and cook for 4 minutes or until tender. Place asparagus on serving plates. Add the tofu and thyme to the pan and cook for 30 seconds on each side or until heated through. Place the tofu on top of the asparagus and serve with the balsamic butter. Serves 2.

squid with green chilli and kaffir lime

12 baby squid, cleaned and halved
1 green chilli, seeded and chopped
4 kaffir lime leaves*, finely shredded
2 tablespoons olive oil
cracked black pepper and sea salt
salad greens, lime and avocado to serve

Place squid in a bowl with chilli, lime leaves, olive oil, pepper and salt, and mix to combine. Preheat a grill or barbecue to high heat. Cook the squid on a hot grill, a few pieces at a time, for 10 seconds on each side or until just charred. Serve with salad greens, lime wedges and avocado. Serves 4.
note – get your fishmonger to clean the squid for you— it's easier and tidier than doing it at home.

lamb with quince glaze

600g (1 1/4 lb) lamb backstrap or eye of loin
1 tablespoon oil
3 tablespoons quince paste*
2/3 cup (5 1/2 fl oz) dry white wine
cracked black pepper

Trim lamb of any fat or sinew. Heat oil in a frying pan over high heat. Add lamb and cook for 1–2 minutes on each side or until well sealed and browned. Remove lamb from pan and place on a plate. Reduce heat to medium and add quince paste, wine and pepper to pan and simmer for 2 minutes or until glaze has thickened slightly. Simmer lamb in the quince glaze for an extra 1 minute on each side or until lamb is cooked to your liking.
Slice lamb into large pieces and serve with the quince glaze and steamed asparagus or salad greens and wedges of a nutty, soft blue-vein cheese. Serves 4.
note – this lamb dish is great served with the rocket (arugula) salad with warm walnut dressing and olives on page134 of the short top + sides chapter.

lamb with quince glaze

white fish with pine nut brown butter

pasta with shredded chicken and fried basil

crisp eggplant salad

white fish with pine nut brown butter

100g (3¹/₂ oz) butter
2 tablespoons lemon juice
3 tablespoons pine nuts, roughly chopped
4 firm white fish fillets, such as blue-eye cod, swordfish etc
steamed greens and lemon wedges to serve

Melt butter in a large frying pan over medium heat until butter is a light golden colour. Add lemon juice and pine nuts and cook for 1 minute.
Add fish to pan and cook for 2 minutes on each side or to your liking. Serve fish on steamed greens with the brown pine nut butter as a sauce and with lemon wedges. Serves 2.
note – great served with the iceberg salad on page 134 of the short top + sides chapter.

pasta with shredded chicken and fried basil

450g (14 oz) fresh pasta*
1 tablespoon olive oil
3 chicken breast fillets, halved
2 tablespoons olive oil, extra
¹/₄ cup basil leaves
125g (4 oz) fetta, chopped
cracked black pepper

Place the pasta in a saucepan of boiling water and cook for 4–5 minutes or until al dente.
While pasta is cooking, heat oil in a large frying pan over medium-high heat. Cook the chicken for 2–3 minutes on each side or until cooked through. Remove, cool slightly and shred the chicken.
Add the extra oil to the pan and heat. Add basil and cook for 2 minutes or until crisp. To serve, drain pasta and toss with the chicken, fetta and pepper. Pour over the oil and fried basil and serve with lemon wedges. Serves 4.

crisp eggplant salad

1 eggplant (aubergine), thinly sliced
olive oil
1 baby cos lettuce, halved
150g (5 oz) marinated fetta with oil, crumbled
2 tablespoons basil leaves, torn
cracked black pepper

Brush eggplant well with olive oil. Place in a frying pan over medium-high heat and cook for 2–3 minutes on each side or until golden and crisp.
Place cos lettuce on serving plates and top with eggplant slices, fetta, basil and pepper. Drizzle with the flavoured oil from the fetta and serve. Serves 2.
note – you may also wish to grill some thinly sliced prosciutto until it is crisp and serve as part of this salad.

pasta with scallops and lemon butter

220g (7 oz) fresh pasta*
60g (2 oz) butter
1 tablespoon oil
2 teaspoons shredded lemon zest
cracked black pepper
10 scallops
1 cup chervil sprigs

Place pasta into a saucepan of boiling water and cook for 4–5 minutes or until al dente.
While pasta is cooking, melt the butter and oil in a frying pan over medium heat. Add lemon rind and pepper and cook for 1 minute or until rind is soft. Add the scallops to the pan and cook for 20–30 seconds on each side or until sealed.
To serve, drain pasta and toss with the chervil. Top with the scallops and the lemon butter sauce. Serves 2.
note – this recipe is also great with prawns or cubes of fish such as salmon instead of the scallops.

pasta with scallops and lemon butter

rocket and parmesan couscous salad

1 cup couscous
2 cups (16 fl oz) chicken or vegetable stock, boiling
2 tablespoons butter
1/4 cup grated parmesan cheese
cracked black pepper
200g (6 1/2 oz) rocket (arugula) leaves, trimmed
4 vine-ripened tomatoes, sliced
3 tablespoons balsamic vinegar

Place couscous in a bowl and pour over the boiling stock.
Top with the butter, cover with plastic wrap, and allow it to
stand for 4 minutes or until the stock has been absorbed.
Stir the couscous with a fork and then stir in the parmesan
and lots of cracked black pepper.
Place rocket and tomatoes on serving plates and sprinkle
with the balsamic vinegar. Serves 4.

balsamic glazed steaks

2 tablespoons olive oil
3 tablespoons balsamic vinegar
cracked black pepper
2 fillet steaks, 2–3cm (3/4 to 1 inch) thick
salad greens, sliced red onion and tomato to serve

Combine the olive oil, balsamic vinegar and pepper in
a shallow dish. Place steaks in the marinade and allow to
stand for 2 minutes on each side.
While steaks are marinating, heat a grill pan or a barbecue
to high heat. Place the salad greens, onion and tomato on
serving plates.
Place steaks in hot pan and cook for 1 minute on each side
or to your liking. Brush with extra marinade while cooking.
Place steaks on top of salad and serve. Serves 2.
note – make sure the steaks are not in the marinade too
long as the acid will change the texture of the meat.

chilli steak wraps

500g (1 lb) rump steak
1–2 tablespoons Asian chilli paste
8 flour tortillas*, warmed
3/4 cup prepared hommus*
8 lettuce leaves
2 tomatoes, chopped
1/2 red onion, chopped
chilli sauce

Trim the steak of any fat or sinew and spread the chilli
paste over the steak. Cook the steak on a preheated hot
grill or barbecue for 1–2 minutes on each side or until
cooked to your liking.
While the steak is cooking, spread the warmed tortillas with
hommus and top with lettuce, tomato and onion. Slice the
steak, place on the salad and top with chilli sauce. Wrap
one end of the bread to enclose the bottom of the filling
and then fold over the sides to enclose. Serves 4.
note – warm the tortillas in the microwave or covered in
a warm oven.

miso soup with chicken and noodles

4 tablespoons white miso paste*
2 teaspoons fish sauce*
2 tablespoons soy sauce
6 cups (48 fl oz) hot water
2 chicken breast fillets, sliced
100g (3 1/2 oz) Asian greens
200g (6 1/2 oz) fresh hokkien noodles*

Place miso, fish sauce, soy and water in a saucepan over
high heat and bring to the boil. Reduce heat to simmer,
add chicken slices and cook for 1 minute. Add greens and
noodles and cook for 2 minutes or until noodles are tender.
To serve, ladle soup into bowls and serve. Serves 4.

rocket and parmesan couscous salad

chilli steak wraps

balsamic glazed steaks

miso soup with chicken and noodles

crisp prawns with iceberg salad

hoisin pork in green onion pancakes

swordfish fried in sage olive oil

crisp prawns with iceberg salad

12–14 medium-sized green (raw) prawns
oil for shallow frying
1 cup rice flour
1 tablespoon ground cumin
2 teaspoons chilli powder
cracked black pepper and sea salt
chopped chilli and extra sea salt to serve
iceberg salad
1 iceberg lettuce heart
3 tablespoons olive oil
2 tablespoons lemon juice
2 teaspoons dijon mustard
cracked black pepper

Rinse prawns and drain. Heat enough oil in a frying pan to shallow fry over high heat. Toss the prawns in combined rice flour, cumin, chilli powder, pepper and sea salt and shake away excess. Place the prawns, a few at a time, in the hot oil and cook for 1 minute on each side or until crisp. Drain on absorbent paper.
To serve, halve the iceberg lettuce and place on serving plates. Combine oil, lemon juice, mustard and pepper and pour over the iceberg lettuce. Sprinkle the prawns with chopped chilli and sea salt and serve with the iceberg lettuce salad. Serves 2.

hoisin pork in green onion pancakes

2 teaspoons sesame oil
600g (1¼ lb) pork fillet
frozen, ready-made green onion pancakes (see note)
6 shallots (green onions), sliced
hoisin sauce*

Heat the oil in a frying pan over medium heat. Add the pork and cook for 3 minutes on each side, or until almost cooked through.
While the pork is cooking, heat the green onion pancakes following the packet directions and keep warm in the oven. To serve, slice the pork. Place a small pile of shallots onto each pancake. Top with the pork and hoisin sauce and roll up the edges to enclose the filling. Serve with steamed greens. Serves 4.
note – green onion pancakes are easily found in the freezer section of Chinese or Asian supermarkets. You can also purchase them already cooked from most Chinese barbecue shops. If you have the time, use the crepe recipe on page 165 of the basics chapter and add ¼ cup of chopped shallots.

swordfish fried in sage olive oil

3 tablespoons fruity olive oil
2 tablespoons sage leaves
2 teaspoons grated lemon rind
cracked black pepper
4 thin swordfish steaks

Heat olive oil in a large frying pan over medium-high heat. Add sage, lemon rind and pepper and cook for 2 minutes or until the sage is crisp.
Add swordfish to the pan and cook for 1 minute on each side or until almost cooked through. Serve the swordfish with the sage oil. Serves 4.
note – this recipe suits any type of firm white fish and is great served with the salt and rosemary baked potatoes on page 134 of the short top + sides chapter.

white bean and tuna salad

125g (4 oz) baby English spinach leaves
375g (12 oz) can cannellini beans, drained
375g (12 oz) can tuna in oil, drained
1 Lebanese cucumber, chopped
2 tomatoes, chopped
2 tablespoons chopped flat-leaf (Italian) parsley
2 tablespoons olive oil
2 tablespoons lemon juice
cracked black pepper

Divide the spinach, beans, tuna, cucumber, tomato and parsley among the serving plates.
Combine the oil, lemon juice and pepper and pour over the salad. Serve with bread. Serves 4.

white bean and tuna salad

peppered beef and cucumber salad

warm tuna panini

prawn salad with parmesan dressing

peppered beef and cucumber salad

550g (1 lb 2 oz) rump or topside steak
oil
cracked black pepper
salad
150g (5 oz) baby English spinach leaves
2 Lebanese cucumbers
2 shallots (green onions), chopped
2 tablespoons chopped flat-leaf (Italian) parsley
2 tablespoons white wine vinegar
1 tablespoon sesame oil

Brush the steak with oil and sprinkle with pepper. Cook on a hot barbecue, under a grill or in a hot frying pan for 1–2 minutes on each side or to your liking. Place the steak on a plate and cover for 2 minutes to rest the meat. While the steak is cooking, place the spinach leaves on serving plates. Slice the cucumbers with a vegetable peeler and combine with shallots, parsley, vinegar and sesame oil. Slice the meat and place on spinach. Top with the cucumber salad and serve. Serves 4.

warm tuna panini

2 round Turkish breads
1/4 cup whole-egg mayonnaise
1 tablespoon lemon juice
1 tablespoon chopped dill
375g (12 oz) can tuna in oil, drained
50g (1 3/4 oz) baby English spinach leaves
1 tomato, sliced
cracked black pepper and sea salt
olive oil

Halve the Turkish bread and spread the bottom halves with the combined mayonnaise, lemon and dill. Top with tuna, spinach, tomato and pepper and salt, and then the Turkish bread tops.
Heat a little olive oil in a frying pan over medium heat. Place sandwiches in frying pan and weight each sandwich with a small plate and something heavy (like a can of tomatoes). Cook for 4 minutes on each side or until golden. Serves 2.

prawn salad with parmesan dressing

550g (1 lb 2 oz) cooked prawns, peeled
1 cos lettuce, separated
1 avocado, quartered
1 tomato, chopped
2 tablespoons salted capers, rinsed
parmesan dressing
1/4 cup grated parmesan cheese
1/2 cup whole-egg mayonnaise
2 tablespoons oil
3 tablespoons lime juice
cracked black pepper

Arrange the prawns, lettuce, avocado, tomato and capers on serving plates.
Combine the parmesan, mayonnaise, oil, lime juice and pepper and pour over the salad.
Serve with bread and extra lime wedges. Serves 4.

chilli pasta with lemon tuna

400g (13 oz) fresh chilli linguini or angel hair pasta*
300g (10 oz) sashimi tuna*
3 tablespoons lemon juice
2 tablespoons oil
1–2 teaspoons wasabi paste*
2 tablespoons chervil sprigs
cracked black pepper

Place the pasta in a large saucepan of boiling water and cook for 4–5 minutes or until al dente.
While the pasta is cooking, chop the tuna into small diced pieces. Combine the lemon juice, oil and wasabi. Drain the pasta and toss with the tuna, chervil and lemon juice mixture. Top with cracked black pepper and serve with a leaf salad. Serves 4.
note – this recipe is just as good with salmon or ocean trout. If fresh pasta is not readily obtainable, use 400g (13 oz) dry pasta, but the recipe will take a little longer than 10 minutes. Serve with the iceberg salad on page 134 of the short top + sides chapter to make a complete meal.

chilli pasta with lemon tuna

spinach salad with warm garlic dressing

grilled honey mustard and smoked ham flatbreads

pasta with chicken and spinach

spinach salad with warm garlic dressing

250g (8 oz) baby English spinach leaves
1/2 cup semi-dried tomatoes*
12 slices sourdough baguette
olive oil
warm garlic dressing
3 tablespoons olive oil
3 cloves garlic, sliced
2 tablespoons salted capers, rinsed
1/4 cup linguarian olives
2 tablespoons lemon juice
2 tablespoons thyme leaves
cracked black pepper

Place the spinach leaves and tomatoes on serving plates. Then place the baguette slices on a tray and drizzle with a little olive oil. Place under a hot grill or grill pan and toast for 1 minute on each side or until golden.
Heat the oil in a saucepan over medium heat. Add the garlic and cook for 1 minute or until lightly browned. Add the capers, olives, lemon juice, thyme and pepper to pan and cook for 1 minute or until heated through. Pour the warm dressing over the salad and top with the grilled baguette. Serves 4.

grilled honey mustard and smoked ham flatbreads

2 tablespoons honey
3 tablespoons dijon mustard
4 flatbreads
6–8 slices double-smoked ham
6–8 slices ripe Brie
4–6 radicchio leaves
olive oil

Combine honey and mustard and spread over 2 flatbreads. Top with the ham, Brie and radicchio. Top with remaining flatbreads and brush with a little olive oil. Place under a hot grill or in a grill pan for 1–2 minutes on each side or until bread is crisp and golden. Serves 2.

pasta with chicken and spinach

450g (14 oz) fresh pasta*
2 1/2 cups bottled tomato pasta sauce or classic tomato sauce (see page 146 of basics chapter)
3 chicken breast fillets, sliced
150g (5 oz) baby English spinach leaves
cracked black pepper
parmesan cheese to serve

Place the pasta into a saucepan of boiling water and cook for 4–5 minutes or until al dente.
While pasta is cooking, heat the tomato sauce in a frying pan over high heat. When the sauce is bubbling, add the chicken slices. Cover and cook for 2–3 minutes or until the chicken is cooked.
To serve, drain the pasta, place on serving plates and top with the spinach leaves. Top with the tomato chicken and serve with pepper and parmesan. Serves 4.

grilled prosciutto sandwiches

4 slices sourdough or Turkish bread
butter
3 bocconcini*, sliced
2 tablespoons basil leaves
8–12 slices prosciutto*
1–2 tablespoons grated parmesan cheese
cracked black pepper
figs and rocket (arugula) leaves to serve

Place sourdough slices under a preheated grill on medium heat and toast one side. Turn the bread and spread with butter. Top with bocconcini, basil, prosciutto, parmesan and pepper and place under the grill for 1 minute or until the parmesan has melted and prosciutto is crisp.
Serve the grilled sandwiches with figs and rocket (arugula) leaves. Serves 4.
note – make a larger meal of these sandwiches by serving with the roast tomato salad on page 134 of the short top + sides chapter.

grilled prosciutto sandwiches

chocolate fudge sauce for ice cream

white chocolate tiramisu

stone fruit and berries in muscato

amaretto french toast

chocolate fudge sauce for ice cream

½ cup (4 fl oz) cream
125g (4 oz) dark chocolate, chopped
vanilla bean, chocolate or toffee ice cream

Place the cream in a saucepan over medium heat and cook until hot. Remove from heat and add the chocolate, stirring until smooth. Cool slightly and pour over your choice of ice cream. Makes 250ml (1 cup).
note – store the excess sauce in the refrigerator and warm gently to reuse.

white chocolate tiramisu

150g (5 oz) thin Italian sponge finger biscuits
¼ cup (2 fl oz) strong espresso, chilled
¼ cup (2 fl oz) coffee liqueur
¾ cup (6 fl oz) thick cream
white chocolate shavings

Pile the sponge finger biscuits onto serving plates. Drizzle with combined espresso and liqueur. Top with the thick cream and white chocolate shavings. Serves 4.

stone fruit and berries in muscato

2 plums, quartered
2 peaches, halved
150g (5 oz) blueberries
150g (5 oz) raspberries
1½ cups (12 fl oz) chilled muscato d'asti wine*

Place the fruit in serving bowls. Top with the well-chilled muscato and serve with a knife, fork and large spoon for the juice. Serves 4.

amaretto french toast

1 egg, lightly beaten
2 tablespoons amaretto
2 tablespoons caster (superfine) sugar
1 teaspoon vanilla extract
½ cup (4 fl oz) milk
3 slices bread, crusts removed and halved

Place the egg, amaretto, sugar and vanilla in a bowl and whisk to combine. Whisk in the milk.
Heat a frying pan over medium heat and grease with a little butter. Dip a few pieces of bread into the egg mixture and place in the hot frying pan. Cook for 2 minutes on each side or until golden. Repeat with the remaining bread. Serve dredged in icing sugar or with maple syrup and small glasses of amaretto and coffee. Serves 2.

figs in vanilla port

¼ cup sugar
¾ cup (6 fl oz) quality port
1 teaspoon vanilla extract
4 figs, halved

Place the sugar, port and vanilla in a frying pan over low heat and stir until the sugar has dissolved. Allow to simmer for 1 minute.
Place figs in serving bowls and pour the vanilla port over them. Serve with thick cream or toffee ice cream. Serves 4.
note – if you have the spare time, make the coconut macaroons on page 126 of the short top + sides chapter and serve them on the side.

figs in vanilla port

20 minutes

frittata

udon soup

laksa

rice pilaf

salads

mash

stir fry

harissa

bruschetta

lentils

fried chicken with goats curd

udon soup with grilled chicken

crisp pancetta baked pork fillet

fried chicken with goats curd

4 chicken breast fillets, skin on
100–150g (3½–5 oz) goats curd
sea salt and cracked black pepper
2 tablespoons oil
2 tablespoons lemon thyme sprigs

Make a pocket in each chicken breast between the skin and the flesh. Fill the pocket with goats curd using a teaspoon or small spatula. Sprinkle the skin of the chicken with sea salt and pepper.
Heat the oil in a frying pan over medium-high heat. Add the lemon thyme sprigs and cook for 1 minute. Place chicken, skin-side down, in pan and cook for 3–4 minutes or until well browned. Turn chicken and cook for 1–2 minutes or until cooked through. Serve the chicken sliced into large pieces with lemon thyme oil from the pan over it and with a simple salad or steamed greens. Serves 4.
note – if goats curd is not your thing, try thick mascarpone instead. Try serving this with the asparagus with balsamic butter on page 134 of the short top + sides chapter.

udon soup with grilled chicken

3 cups (24 fl oz) chicken stock
2 tablespoons miso paste*
300g (10 oz) fresh udon noodles*
2 chicken breasts, sliced
oil
2 shallots (green onions), sliced
80g (2¾ oz) enoki mushrooms

Place the chicken stock and miso in a saucepan over high heat and bring to the boil. Reduce heat, allow to simmer and add the udon noodles.
Brush the chicken slices with oil and cook under a hot grill or in a grill pan for 1 minute on each side.
Add the shallots and mushrooms to the soup and ladle into bowls. Top with the grilled chicken and serve. Serves 2.

crisp pancetta baked pork fillet

12–14 slices pancetta*
350–400g (11–13 oz) pork fillet
1 apple, sliced
2 teaspoons oil
2 tablespoons sage leaves
cracked black pepper

Preheat oven to 220°C (425°F). Wrap the pancetta around the pork fillet to enclose. Place the sliced apple in the base of a baking dish and top with the pork. Sprinkle with the oil, sage and pepper.
Bake in the oven for 12–15 minutes or until the pork is cooked to your liking. Serve the pork thickly sliced with a peppery rocket (arugula) salad. Serves 2.
note – this recipe is also great with the pork wrapped in thinly sliced prosciutto. Accompany this with the roast garlic mash on page 134 of the short top + sides chapter.

salt and five spice chicken

400g (13 oz) chicken pieces
2 tablespoons lemon juice
1 tablespoon chilli oil
pinch of Chinese five spive powder*
1 tablespoon sea salt
1 teaspoon five spice powder*, extra

Place the chicken pieces in a bowl with the lemon, chilli oil and the pinch of five spice powder and allow to stand for 5 minutes.
Preheat oven to 200°C (400°F). Then heat a large frying pan over high heat. Add the chicken pieces, skin-side down, and cook for 2 minutes on each side or until crisp and golden. Place the chicken on a baking tray and bake in the oven for 8–10 minutes or until cooked through.
Combine the salt and extra five spice powder and serve in small piles with the chicken. To serve, dip small pieces of the chicken in the salt and five spice mixture and serve with rice and greens. Serves 2.

salt and five spice chicken

sweet chilli prawn cakes

grilled tomato bruschetta salad

coconut and salmon laksa

sweet chilli prawn cakes

600g (1¼ lb) green (raw) prawn meat
1 egg white
2 kaffir lime leaves*, shredded
3 tablespoons sweet chilli sauce
2 cups fresh breadcrumbs
3 tablespoons rice flour
oil for shallow frying
extra sweet chilli sauce to serve

Place prawn meat, egg white, lime leaves, sweet chilli sauce, breadcrumbs and rice flour in a food processor and process until the mixture is combined but not smooth. With wetted hands, shape the mixture into small cakes. Heat enough oil in a frying pan over medium-high heat to shallow fry. Add the prawn cakes a few at a time and cook for 3 minutes on each side or until golden. Drain and serve with extra sweet chilli sauce and salad greens. Serves 4.
note – these prawn cakes are a great small bite to serve with drinks. Shape the cakes and refrigerate, then shallow fry them just before serving.

grilled tomato bruschetta salad

2 tomatoes, halved
4 slices Italian crusty bread
cracked black pepper
olive oil
1 clove garlic, halved
50g (1¾ oz) rocket (arugula) leaves
50g (1¾ oz) baby English spinach leaves
balsamic vinegar and olive oil for a dressing
shaved parmesan cheese to serve

Place the tomatoes and bread on a tray, sprinkle with pepper and drizzle with oil. Place under a preheated hot grill. Cook bread for 1 minute, turn and cook for a further minute or until golden. Remove the bread and continue cooking the tomatoes for a further 10 minutes or until soft. Rub both sides of the bread with the garlic clove.
Place the rocket and spinach leaves on serving plates and top with the bruschetta and tomatoes. Finish with combined balsamic vinegar and olive oil, then top with parmesan cheese. Serves 2.
note – you can also omit the bruschetta from this recipe and place the tomato, rocket and spinach salad in the parmesan shortcrust pastry shell on page 173 of the basics chapter.

coconut and salmon laksa

150g (5 oz) dry rice vermicelli
4 tablespoons quality laksa paste*
1 tablespoon shredded ginger
1 kaffir lime leaf*, shredded (optional)
3½ cups (28 fl oz) fish or vegetable stock
2 cups (16 fl oz) coconut milk
250g (8 oz) salmon fillet, chopped
4 baby bok choy, leaves separated
chopped red chillies and coriander leaves to serve

Place the rice noodles in a bowl of boiling water and stand for 2 minutes, drain and set aside.
Place the laksa paste, ginger and lime leaf in a saucepan over medium-high heat and cook for 1 minute or until fragrant. Add the stock and coconut milk and reduce the temperature to low.
When the coconut broth is hot, add salmon and bok choy and cook for 1–2 minutes. Place rice noodles in the bottom of serving bowls and ladle broth over the top. Sprinkle with chopped chillies and coriander leaves. Serves 4.

peppered garfish with lemon rice pilaf

4 garfish, butterflied
oil
cracked black pepper and sea salt
lemon rice pilaf
1 tablespoon oil
1 onion, chopped
1½ cups long-grain rice
3 cups (24 fl oz) vegetable or chicken stock
2–3 tablespoons lemon juice
2 tablespoons chopped flat-leaf (Italian) parsley
cracked black pepper and sea salt

To cook the pilaf, heat oil in a saucepan over medium heat. Add the onion and cook for 2 minutes or until soft. Add the rice and cook for 1 minute. Add the stock to pan and cook for 10–12 minutes or until tunnels have formed in the rice and almost all the stock has been absorbed. Stir through the lemon juice and the parsley, pepper and sea salt.
While the pilaf is cooking, brush the garfish with oil. Sprinkle with pepper and sea salt. Heat a frying pan over high heat and cook the garfish for 2–3 minutes on each side or until it has a crisp skin and is cooked through. Serve with the lemon pilaf. Serves 2.

peppered garfish with lemon rice pilaf

spiced chicken with chilli pilaf

2 tablespoons oil

3 red chillies, seeded and chopped

1½ cups rice

3 cups (24 fl oz) chicken stock

150g (5 oz) snake beans, halved

spiced chicken

2 tablespoons oil, extra

4 chicken breast fillets, halved

2 tablespoons ground cumin

2 teaspoons ground cinnamon

cracked black pepper

To make the chilli pilaf, place the oil in a saucepan over medium-high heat. Add the chilli and cook for 1 minute. Add the rice and cook for a further 1 minute. Add the stock and bring to the boil. Reduce heat and allow the rice to simmer for 10–12 minutes or until almost all liquid has been absorbed. Place the snake beans on top of the rice, cover tightly and remove from heat.

While rice is cooking, heat extra oil in a frying pan. Toss the chicken pieces with the combined cumin, cinnamon and pepper and cook for 2 minutes on each side or until golden. Serve chicken with snake beans and chilli pilaf. Serves 4.

grilled fennel salad

4 baby fennel bulbs, halved

150g (5 oz) goats cheese, sliced

1 tablespoon thyme leaves

olive oil

cracked black pepper

180g (6 oz) baby rocket (arugula) leaves

150g (5 oz) cherry tomatoes, quartered

balsamic vinegar and olive oil to serve

Place the fennel, cut-side up, on a baking tray. Top the fennel with goats cheese, thyme and a little olive oil. Place under a hot preheated grill for 5 minutes or until the fennel has softened but is still firm.

To serve, place rocket leaves and tomatoes on serving plates and top with the grilled fennel. Serve with the balsamic vinegar and olive oil as a dressing and with slices of grain bread. Serves 4.

lemon and parsley fried fish

2 tablespoons finely grated lemon rind

¼ cup chopped flat-leaf (Italian) parsley

cracked black pepper and sea salt

4 fillets of white fish

olive oil

lemon wedges to serve

greens to serve

Combine the lemon rind, parsley, pepper and salt in a bowl. Press the lemon and parsley mixture onto both sides of the fish. Heat a little olive oil in a large frying pan over high heat. Cook the fish for 1–2 minutes on each side or until cooked to your liking. Serve with lemon wedges and steamed greens. Serves 4.

stir fry beef, ginger and greens

1 tablespoon sesame oil

2 tablespoons shredded ginger

2 cloves garlic, sliced

500g (1 lb) rump steak, sliced

500g (1 lb) Asian greens, trimmed and halved

2 tablespoons oyster sauce

½ cup (4 fl oz) Chinese cooking wine*

2 teaspoons cornflour

¼ cup sliced garlic chives

Heat the sesame oil in a wok or frying pan over high heat. Add the ginger and the garlic and cook for 1 minute or until soft. Add the beef and stir fry for 2–3 minutes or until the beef is well browned and sealed.

Add the choy sum or gai larn to pan with the oyster sauce and cooking wine and stir fry for 2 minutes. Mix cornflour with a little water to form a smooth paste. Add to the pan and stir fry for 2 minutes or until greens are tender and the sauce has thickened. Sprinkle with garlic chives and serve with rice or rice noodles. Serves 4.

spiced chicken with chilli pilaf

lemon and parsley fried fish

grilled fennel salad

stir fry beef, ginger and greens

veal with tomato and bocconcini   bacon and broad bean soup

chicken simmered in soy and star anise

veal with tomato and bocconcini

1 tablespoon oil
4 veal steaks
4 slices crusty bread
4 small bocconcini*, sliced
2 tomatoes, sliced
olive oil
shredded basil

Heat oil in a frying pan over high heat. Add veal and cook for 1 minute on each side or until sealed. Place veal and bread on a tray, top the veal with bocconcini and tomato and drizzle both the veal and bread with a little olive oil. Cook the veal and bread under a hot preheated grill for 2–3 minutes or until the bread is toasted and bocconcini has started to melt. To serve, place a little shredded basil on the bread, top with the veal then a little more basil. Serve with a simple green salad. Serves 4.

bacon and broad bean soup

2 teaspoons oil
2 leeks, chopped
2 tablespoons rosemary leaves
6 rashers bacon, rind removed and sliced
2 x 440g (14 oz) cans peeled tomatoes, lightly crushed
1 cup (8 fl oz) red wine
2 cups (16 fl oz) beef stock
1½ cups broad beans
cracked black pepper and sea salt

Heat the oil in a large saucepan over medium heat. Add the leek, rosemary and bacon and cook for 5 minutes or until the leek is soft. Add tomatoes, wine and stock and allow to simmer for 8 minutes.
Add the broad beans to soup and cook for 5 minutes or until tender. Season with pepper and sea salt and serve soup with bread. Serves 4.
note – use frozen broad beans if fresh are unavailable.

chicken simmered in soy and star anise

⅓ cup (2¾ fl oz) soy sauce
¼ cup (2 fl oz) Chinese cooking wine* or sherry
2 tablespoons oyster sauce
2 star anise*
1 cinnamon stick
2 tablespoons brown sugar
2 chicken breast fillets
1 bunch bok choy or Chinese greens, trimmed and halved

Place the soy, cooking wine or sherry, oyster sauce, star anise, cinnamon stick and sugar in a frying pan over high heat and bring to the boil. Add the chicken and cook for 3 minutes on each side. Add the greens to the pan and cook for 2 minutes or until tender.
Place chicken and greens on serving plates and spoon over the pan juices as sauce. Serve with steamed rice. Serves 2.

pasta with rocket and blue cheese

450g (14 oz) fresh* or dry pasta
2 tablespoons butter
½ cup walnuts
2 tablespoons cider vinegar
3 tablespoons chopped chives
180g (6 oz) baby rocket (arugula) leaves
150g (5 oz) blue cheese, sliced
cracked black pepper

Place the pasta in a saucepan of boiling water and cook until al dente.
While the pasta is cooking, heat butter in a small frying pan over medium heat. Add the walnuts and cook for 2 minutes or until fragrant. Add the cider vinegar to the pan. Drain the pasta and toss with the chives, rocket, blue cheese, walnut dressing and cracked black pepper.
Serve the pasta with bread and a tomato salad in a simple balsamic dressing. Serves 4.

pasta with rocket and blue cheese

parmesan crusted chicken

grilled eggplant with basil salsa verde

garlic beef with spiced couscous

chicken poached in coconut curry

parmesan crusted chicken

2 chicken breast fillets
2 egg whites, lightly beaten
1 cup grated parmesan cheese
cracked black pepper
2 tablespoons oil
2 ripe tomatoes, sliced
2 tablespoons shredded basil
balsamic vinegar and olive oil to serve

Cut each chicken fillet into 2 thin, flat pieces. Dip each piece in the egg white and then press the chicken in the combined parmesan and pepper.
Heat the oil over medium-high heat and add the chicken pieces. Cook for 1–2 minutes on each side or until the chicken is golden and cooked through.
To serve, place tomato and basil on serving plates and top with balsamic and olive oil then the slices of chicken. Serve with lemon wedges and bread. Serves 2.

garlic beef with spiced couscous

1 tablespoon oil
3 cloves garlic, sliced
2 sirloin steaks
spiced couscous
1 cup couscous
1½ cups (12 fl oz) chicken stock, boiling
2 tablespoons butter
2 teaspoons cumin seeds
2 tablespoons chopped coriander
cracked black pepper and sea salt

To make the spiced couscous, place the couscous and stock in a bowl. Cover tightly with plastic wrap and allow to stand for 4–5 minutes or until the stock has been absorbed. While the couscous is standing, heat the butter in a frying pan over medium heat. Add the cumin seeds and cook for 2 minutes. Then add the couscous, coriander, pepper and sea salt and cook for 1 minute or until heated through.
To cook the steak, heat oil in a frying pan over high heat. Press the garlic slices into the steaks and place in the hot pan. Cook for 2 minutes on each side or to your liking. Serve steak on couscous with steamed greens. Serves 2.

grilled eggplant with basil salsa verde

2 eggplants (aubergines), halved
3 tomatoes, halved
basil salsa verde
⅓ cup chopped flat-leaf (Italian) parsley
⅔ cup chopped basil
2 cloves garlic, sliced
1 tablespoon dijon mustard
3 tablespoons capers
⅓ cup (2¾ fl oz) olive oil
2 tablespoons lemon juice

Cut deep slits into the eggplants and the tomatoes and place on a baking tray.
To make the basil salsa verde, place the parsley, basil, garlic, mustard and capers into a food processor or a blender and process until finely chopped. Add the olive oil and lemon juice and process until a smooth paste forms. Spread the basil salsa verde over the eggplant and tomatoes. Place under a preheated hot grill and cook for 5 minutes or until eggplant is soft. Serve with grilled flatbreads and firm goats cheese. Serves 4.

chicken poached in coconut curry

3 tablespoons red curry paste*
6 chicken thigh fillets, halved
2 cups chopped sweet potato
2 cups (16 fl oz) chicken stock
1½ cups (12 fl oz) coconut milk
¼ cup coriander leaves

Place a frying pan over medium-high heat and add the curry paste. Cook for 1–2 minutes or until the paste is fragrant. Add the chicken and sweet potato to the pan and cook for 2 minutes. Add the stock and coconut milk and reduce heat to low. Allow to simmer gently for 12 minutes or until chicken and sweet potato are cooked.
Sprinkle coriander over the chicken and serve with steamed rice or with steamed greens. Serves 4.
note – do not boil the coconut milk as it will separate—the flavour will be the same but the appearance and texture of the sauce will be different.

hokkien noodles with sesame chicken

500g (1 lb) fresh hokkien noodles*
2 teaspoons sesame oil
2 onions, chopped
3–4 chicken breast fillets, sliced
3 tablespoons soy sauce
½ cup (4 fl oz) Chinese cooking wine* or dry sherry
2 tablespoons white miso paste*
2 cups greens, such as spinach or bok choy
1 tablespoon sesame seeds

Wash the noodles under hot water to separate, then drain and set aside. Heat the oil in a frying pan or wok over high heat. Add the onion and cook for 2 minutes. Place the chicken in pan and cook for 4 minutes or until well browned. Add the soy, wine, miso, greens and hokkien noodles to pan and cook for 4 minutes or until greens are tender. To serve, place in serving bowls and sprinkle with sesame seeds. Serves 4.

lime leaf and chilli lentils

1 tablespoon oil
4 medium red chillies, chopped
2 tablespoons shredded ginger
5 kaffir lime leaves*, shredded
1½ cups red lentils
3 cups (24 fl oz) vegetable or chicken stock
1 cup Thai basil leaves*
½ cup coriander leaves
steamed snake beans to serve

Heat the oil in a frying pan over medium heat. Add the chillies, ginger and lime leaves and cook for 1 minute. Add the lentils and stock to the pan, cook for 5–6 minutes or until the lentils are cooked but firm.
Place the basil and coriander in serving bowls and top with lentils. Serve with steamed snake beans. Serves 4.

pork cutlets with ginger sweet potato mash

2 pork cutlets
sesame seeds
oil
ginger sweet potato mash
400g (13 oz) sweet potato, peeled and chopped
2 tablespoons shredded ginger
30g (1 oz) butter
1 tablespoon honey
milk
2 tablespoons coriander leaves

To make the mash, place the sweet potato and ginger in a saucepan of boiling water and cook for 5–7 minutes or until tender; drain. Mash the sweet potato with the butter, honey and enough milk to make it smooth. Stir coriander through the mash.
While the sweet potato is cooking, press the pork cutlets in the sesame seeds and coat each side. Heat oil in a frying pan over medium heat and cook pork for 2–3 minutes on each side or until golden and cooked to your liking. Serve with mash and steamed greens. Serves 2.
note – this is great served with the asparagus with balsamic butter on page 134 of the short top + sides chapter.

salad of lamb noodles and peanuts

200g (6½ oz) dry cellophane (beanthread) noodles*
1 tablespoon chilli oil*
1 clove garlic, chopped
500g (1 lb) tender lamb strips
150g (5 oz) snow peas, shredded
½ red capsicum, sliced
3 tablespoons soy sauce
2 tablespoons sweet chilli sauce
¼ cup coriander leaves
½ cup roasted unsalted peanuts, roughly chopped

Place cellophane noodles in a bowl and cover with boiling water. Allow to stand for 4 minutes or until soft; drain. Heat the chilli oil in a wok or frying pan over high heat. Add the garlic and cook for 30 seconds. Add the lamb and stir fry for 3 minutes or until sealed. Add the snow peas and capsicum and stir fry for 2 minutes. Then add the soy sauce and sweet chilli and remove from heat. Toss the stir fry with the noodles, coriander leaves and peanuts. Place onto serving plates and serve with wedges of lime. Serves 4.

hokkien noodles with sesame chicken

pork cutlets with ginger sweet potato mash

lime leaf and chilli lentils

salad of lamb noodles and peanuts

soy quail stir fry

figs baked on haloumi

warmed olive and garlic pasta

soy quail stir fry

2 teaspoons sesame oil
4 quails, quartered
1/3 cup (2¾ fl oz) salt-reduced soy sauce
1/3 cup (2¾ fl oz) Chinese cooking wine* or dry sherry
2 tablespoons oyster sauce
2 tablespoons brown sugar
6 shallots (green onions), sliced
150g (5 oz) shiitake mushrooms*, sliced
150g (5 oz) snow peas, halved
noodles to serve

Heat oil in a wok or frying pan over high heat. Add the quail and stir fry for 5 minutes or until well browned. Add the soy, wine, oyster sauce and sugar and cook for 2–3 minutes or until the sauce has reduced by half.
Add the shallots, mushrooms and snow peas to the pan and cook for 2 minutes or until tender. Serve the quail on stir-fried hot noodles. Serves 4.

figs baked on haloumi

8 figs, halved
4 long slices prosciutto*, halved lengthwise
60g (2 oz) soft butter
cracked black pepper
8 slices haloumi*

Preheat the oven to 220°C (425°F). Wrap each fig with prosciutto, place a little butter on the top of each fig and sprinkle with pepper.
Place the slices of haloumi on a baking tray and top each one with two wrapped figs. Bake in the oven for 12 minutes, or until the prosciutto is crisp and figs are soft. Place on a serving plate and serve with a salad of greens. Serves 4.
note – you can also adapt this recipe to a tart. Place the haloumi and wrapped figs, uncooked, in a blind-baked shortcrust pastry shell (see page 170 of the basics chapter) and then bake for 12 minutes in the pastry shell. Serve with a salad of green leaves.

warmed olive and garlic pasta

450g (14 oz) fresh* or dry pasta
2 tablespoons olive oil
1 cup fresh breadcrumbs
1 tablespoon olive oil, extra
3 cloves garlic, sliced
2 tablespoons rosemary leaves
2 teaspoons shredded lemon rind
1 cup of your favourite olives
cracked black pepper

Place the pasta into a saucepan of boiling water and cook for 4–5 minutes (for fresh pasta) or 8–12 minutes (for dried pasta) or until al dente, and drain.
While the pasta is cooking, heat the oil in a frying pan over high heat. Add the breadcrumbs and toast them, stirring, for 2–3 minutes or until golden. Set aside. Wipe the pan clean and heat extra oil. Add garlic and cook for 1 minute or until lightly golden. Add the rosemary, lemon, olives and pepper and cook for 2–3 minutes or until warmed through. To serve, toss the olive mixture through the warm pasta and top with toasted breadcrumbs. Serve with green salad. Serves 4.
note – instead of topping with toasted breadcrumbs, serve with the sesame sweet potatoes on page 134 of the short top + sides chapter as shown in the cover photograph.

basil frittata with gravlax

4 eggs, lightly beaten
1/2 cup (4 fl oz) milk
1/3 cup shredded basil
1/3 cup grated aged cheddar
cracked black pepper
6–8 slices gravlax*

Place eggs, milk, basil, cheddar and pepper in a bowl and mix to combine. Pour mixture into a nonstick, 20cm frying pan and cook on medium heat for 4 minutes or until the frittata is almost set. Place under a hot grill for 1 minute or until golden. Remove from pan and cut into wedges. Top with gravlax and serve. Serves 2.

basil frittata with gravlax

barbecue pork san choy bau

2 teaspoons sesame oil

2 tablespoons shredded ginger

4 shallots (green onions), sliced

500g (1 lb) Chinese barbecue pork*, sliced

2 tablespoons hoisin sauce*

2 tablespoons soy sauce

bean sprouts

iceberg lettuce cups

extra hoisin sauce to serve

Heat the oil in a frying pan or wok over medium-high heat. Add the ginger and the shallots and cook for 1 minute. Add the pork, hoisin and soy and cook for 3 minutes or until heated through.
To serve, place a small pile of bean sprouts in each lettuce leaf. Top with the barbecue pork mixture and serve with extra hoisin sauce. Serves 4.

warm pork and fennel salad

1 tablespoon oil

650g (1 lb 5 oz) pork fillet, trimmed

4 small fennel bulbs, sliced

1 cup (8 fl oz) dry white wine

cracked black pepper

2 tablespoons rosemary leaves

125g (4 oz) baby English spinach leaves

Heat the oil in a frying pan over medium heat. Add the pork and cook for 2 minutes on each side or until well browned and sealed. Remove the pork from the pan and set aside. Add the fennel, wine, pepper and rosemary to the pan. Cover the frying pan and cook for 6 minutes. Top the fennel with the pork and cook, covered, for a further 6 minutes or until the pork is cooked to your liking. Serve the pork sliced with the baby spinach, fennel and pan juices. Serves 4.

harissa fried fish with warm coriander potatoes

4 x 150g (5 oz) fillets or pieces white fish, such as blue-eye cod or swordfish etc

2–3 tablespoons harissa*

1 tablespoon oil

warm coriander potatoes

500g (1 lb) boiling potatoes, such as kipfler

2 cloves garlic, crushed

1/2 cup thick plain yoghurt

2 tablespoons chopped mint

2 tablespoons chopped coriander

cracked black pepper and sea salt

To make the warm coriander potatoes, halve potatoes, place them in a saucepan of boiling water and cook for 15 minutes or until soft. Drain and allow to cool slightly. While potatoes are cooking, spread the fish with the harrisa. Heat oil in a nonstick frying pan over medium-high heat. Cook the fish for 2–3 minutes on each side or to your liking. Combine the garlic, yoghurt, mint, coriander and pepper and salt and toss through the potatoes. Place on a serving plate and top with the harrisa fried fish. Serves 4.
note – great served with the roast garlic mashed potatoes on page 134 of the short top + sides chapter.

honey lamb kebabs

400g (13 oz) lean lamb loin or fillets

2 tablespoons honey

2 teaspoons grated lemon rind

1 tablespoon rosemary leaves

cracked black pepper

couscous and baby English spinach to serve

Cut lamb into strips or cubes and thread onto skewers. Combine the honey, lemon rind, rosemary and pepper and spread over the kebabs. Place under a hot preheated grill and cook for 1–2 minutes on each side or until cooked to your liking.
Serve the kebabs on couscous and with baby English spinach. Serves 2.
note – you can also serve these kebabs with the sesame sweet potato on page 134 of the short top + sides chapter.

barbecue pork san choy bau

harissa fried fish with warm coriander potatoes

warm pork and fennel salad

honey lamb kebabs

pink apple tarts   caramelised strawberry shortcake

waffles with vanilla espresso syrup

pink apple tarts

2 sheets ready-rolled puff pastry
2 pink lady or sweet red apples
brown sugar

Preheat the oven to 220°C (425°F). Trim 1cm from the edges of the pastry and cut each sheet into 2 pieces. Core the apples and slice thinly.
Place the pastry on baking trays lined with nonstick baking paper and top the pastry with a layer of apples down the middle. Sprinkle the apples with brown sugar. Bake in the oven for 12 minutes or until puffed and golden. Serve with thick cream or ice cream. Serves 4.

caramelised strawberry shortcake

500g (1 lb) strawberries
1/2 cup caster (superfine) sugar
4 good-quality shortbread biscuits
thick cream or ice cream to serve

Remove stalks from the strawberries. Wash strawberries and drain. Place the sugar on a plate and roll strawberries in the sugar to coat lightly.
Heat a nonstick frying pan over high heat. Cook the strawberries for 2 minutes or until they are warm and the sugar has dissolved. Remove strawberries from the pan and set aside. Cook the remaining syrup for 2 minutes.
To serve, place the shortbread on serving plates, top with the warm strawberries and then the warm strawberry sauce and serve with thick cream or ice cream. Serve immediately. Serves 4.

waffles with vanilla espresso syrup

8 waffles
thick cream or ice cream to serve
vanilla espresso syrup
1 cup (8 fl oz) freshly brewed strong espresso
3/4 cup caster (superfine) sugar
2 teaspoons vanilla extract

To make the syrup, place the espresso, sugar and vanilla in a saucepan and stir over low heat until the sugar has dissolved. Increase heat and simmer rapidly for 8 minutes or until the liquid is syrupy.
To serve, warm or toast the waffles and place on serving plates. Pour the vanilla espresso syrup over them and serve with thick cream or vanilla bean or espresso ice cream. Serves 4.

little chocolate brownies

150g (5 oz) butter, softened
1 cup caster (superfine) sugar
3/4 cup cocoa
2 eggs
1 cup self-raising (self-rising) flour

Preheat the oven to 180°C (350°F). Place the butter and sugar in a bowl and beat until light and fluffy. Add cocoa, eggs and flour and mix until combined. Spoon the mixture into nine nonstick 1/2 cup (4 fl oz) capacity muffin tins. Bake in the oven for 10–12 minutes or until cooked but soft in the centre. Invert cakes onto serving plates and serve warm with thick cream or ice cream. Makes 9 cakes.

little chocolate brownies

coconut poached pears

2 cups (16 fl oz) coconut milk
1/3 cup sugar
1 cinnamon stick
4 small soft pears, peeled and halved

Place the coconut milk, sugar and cinnamon in a saucepan over medium-low heat. Do not let the coconut milk boil as it will separate.
Add the pears and cook for 15 minutes, turning once.
To serve, place the pears in bowls and serve warm with the coconut broth. Serves 4.

vanilla simmered quince

2 cups (16 fl oz) water
1 cup sugar
1 vanilla bean, split
1 quince, peeled and sliced

Place the water, sugar and vanilla bean in a frying pan over high heat and stir until the sugar has dissolved. Add the quince to the pan, cover and simmer for 12 minutes or until the quince is tender. Serve with some of the simmering liquid. Serves 2.

chocolate and hazelnut pastries

1 sheet ready-rolled puff pastry
1/4 cup chopped dark chocolate
1/2 teaspoon ground cinnamon
2 tablespoons chopped roasted hazelnuts

Preheat the oven to 200°C (400°F). Trim edges of pastry and cut the sheet into 4 long pieces. Cover half of each piece with the chocolate and sprinkle with cinnamon and hazelnuts, leaving a 1cm (1/2 inch) border on the edge.
Fold over the pastry to enclose and place on a baking tray. Bake in the oven for 15 minutes or until puffed and golden. Serve warm or cold. Serves 4.

steamed coconut custards

3/4 cup (6 fl oz) coconut milk
1 1/4 cups (10 fl oz) cream
3 tablespoons caster (superfine) sugar
4 egg yolks
1 teaspoon finely grated lime rind

Place the coconut milk, cream, caster sugar and egg yolks in a bowl and whisk to combine. Stir the lime rind through. Pour the mixture into 4 ramekins or Chinese tea cups and place in a bamboo steamer. Steam over boiling water for 6–8 minutes or until just beginning to set. Stand for 5 minutes before serving. Serves 4.

coconut poached pears

chocolate and hazelnut pastries

vanilla simmered quince

steamed coconut custards

minutes

risotto

pizza

tempura

rice paper rolls

soup

rosti

soft polenta

corn cakes

salsa verde

steamed chicken

star anise duck salad

sesame beef rice paper rolls

angel hair niçoise

star anise duck salad

4 duck breasts, trimmed of fat
1/3 cup (2¾ fl oz) red wine
1/3 cup (2¾ fl oz) chicken stock
2 star anise*
6 shallots (green onions), sliced
175g (6 oz) mizuna or Asian salad greens

Place duck breasts, skin-side down, in a preheated frying pan over high heat and cook for 10 minutes or until skin is well browned and crisp. Remove the duck from pan and drain the pan of fat. Add the red wine, stock and star anise and cook for 5 minutes or until liquid has reduced by half. Return the duck to the pan, uncooked-side down, and rest in the pan over medium heat for 4 minutes.
Combine the shallots and mizuna or greens and place them on serving plates. Slice the duck and place on top of the greens and pour over the pan sauce from the duck as a warm dressing. Serves 4.

sesame beef rice paper rolls

1 tablespoon oil
400g (13 oz) rump steak
1 tablespoon sesame oil
1 tablespoon soy sauce
2 bunches English spinach, leaves only
2 tablespoons sesame seeds
12 rice paper rounds*
100g (3½ oz) snow pea sprouts
soy sauce for dipping

Heat the oil in a frying pan over high heat. Add the steak and cook for 2–3 minutes on each side or to your liking. Set aside for 2 minutes then slice the steak thinly and place in a bowl with sesame oil and soy.
Place the spinach leaves in a saucepan of boiling water and cook for 5 seconds then drain and squeeze any excess liquid from the spinach. Roughly chop the spinach and combine with the sesame seeds.
Dip the rice paper rounds in hot water for 5–10 seconds or until soft. Remove and pat dry. Place the beef, spinach and snow pea sprouts down the centre of the rice paper. Fold one end over the filling to form a base then roll the rice paper from the side to enclose. Repeat with the remaining mixture and serve with the soy sauce. Serves 4.

angel hair niçoise

400g (13 oz) fresh angel hair pasta*
2 tablespoons chilli oil*
350g (11 oz) tuna steaks
3 tablespoons lime juice
2 tablespoons olive oil
1 clove garlic, crushed
6 anchovy fillets, chopped
200g (6½ oz) green beans, blanched
¾ cup olives
¼ cup roughly chopped flat-leaf (Italian) parsley

Place the angel hair pasta in a large saucepan of boiling water over high heat and cook until al dente.
While pasta is cooking, heat a frying pan over high heat. Add the chilli oil and tuna steaks to pan and sear the tuna for 1 minute on each side. Remove the tuna from pan and slice into pieces. Reduce the pan heat to low, add lime juice, olive oil, garlic and anchovies and cook for 1 minute. Drain the pasta and place in a bowl with tuna, beans, olives and parsley. Pour the warm dressing from the pan over pasta and toss to combine. Serves 4.

lentil and pancetta soup

1 tablespoon oil
2 leeks, chopped
8 slices pancetta*, chopped
400g (13 oz) brown lentils
6 cups (48 fl oz) chicken or vegetable stock
extra pancetta*
cracked black pepper and sea salt

Heat the oil in a saucepan over medium heat. Add the leeks and pancetta and cook for 3 minutes. Add the lentils and stock to the pan and bring to the boil. Allow the soup to boil rapidly for 15–18 minutes or until lentils are soft. While soup is cooking, place a few slices of pancetta under a hot grill and cook for 1 minute on each side or until crisp. To serve, season the soup with pepper and salt and ladle into bowls. Serve topped with the crisp pancetta and lemon wedges to be squeezed over the soup, or a spoonful of crème fraîche. Serves 4.
note – for something a little different to bread, serve the soup with the plain garlic bruschetta on page 126 of the short top + sides chapter.

lentil and pancetta soup

rocket, chicken and pine nut tabouli

fried bug-tails on garlic spinach

chickens baked with quince paste and prosciutto

rocket, chicken and pine nut tabouli

¾ cup cracked wheat
1½ cups (12 fl oz) boiling water
1 tablespoon oil
3 chicken breast fillets
250g (8 oz) rocket (arugula) leaves
¾ cup flat-leaf (Italian) parsley, chopped
¾ cup mint, chopped
200g (6½ oz) cherry tomatoes, quartered
½ cup pine nuts, toasted
3 tablespoons lemon juice
3 tablespoons olive oil
cracked black pepper and sea salt
lemon wedges to serve

Combine the wheat and boiling water in a bowl. Stand for 5 minutes or until wheat has absorbed all water and is soft. Heat the oil in a frying pan over medium-high heat. Add the chicken to the pan and cook for 5 minutes on each side or until cooked through, then set aside to cool.
Place the wheat, rocket, parsley, mint, tomatoes and pine nuts in a bowl. Slice the chicken and add to the salad with combined lemon juice, olive oil, pepper and salt and toss to combine. Serve with lemon wedges. Serves 4.

fried bug-tails on garlic spinach

4 green (raw) Balmain or Moreton Bay bug-tails
rice flour
¼ cup sage leaves
oil for shallow frying
garlic spinach
2 bunches (650g or 1 lb 5 oz) English spinach
75g (2½ oz) butter
2–3 cloves garlic, chopped
lemon wedges to serve

To make garlic spinach, remove the leaves from the stalks and plunge in a saucepan of boiling water for 3 seconds. Drain, squeeze excess liquid from spinach, then set aside. Remove meat in one piece from the shell. Toss meat lightly in rice flour and shake away excess. Heat a frying pan over medium-high heat with enough oil to shallow fry. Add the bug-tails and cook for 1–2 minutes on each side or until golden and crisp; drain on absorbent paper. Add sage to the oil and cook for 1 minute or until crisp, and then drain. To finish, heat the butter and garlic in a frying pan over medium heat and cook for 1 minute. Add the spinach and toss to coat. Top with the fried bug-tails and sage and serve with lemon wedges. Serves 4.

chickens baked with quince paste and prosciutto

4 x 300g (10 oz) small poussins (baby chickens)
4 bay leaves
2 teaspoons fennel seeds
30g (1 oz) quince paste*
16 slices prosciutto*
4 leeks, halved
olive oil
cracked black pepper and sea salt
1 cup (8 fl oz) dry white wine

Preheat the oven to 240°C (475°F). Place a bay leaf and some fennel seeds in the cavity of each chicken. Tie the legs with string to secure. Top the breast of the chickens with quince paste. Wrap prosciutto slices around the chickens and tuck under to secure.
Place the halved leeks in the base of a baking dish and drizzle with a little olive oil and then sprinkle with pepper and sea salt. Pour the wine into the base of the baking dish and then top the leeks with the chickens.
Bake for 20 minutes or until the chicken is cooked through. Serve with the roasted leeks and steamed greens or a green salad. Serves 4.

rare tuna spring rolls with lime and soy

500g (1 lb) piece sashimi tuna*
1 tablespoon wasabi paste*
2 tablespoons coriander leaves
2 tablespoons chopped parsley
8 spring roll wrappers
oil for deep frying
2 tablespoons lime juice
2 tablespoons soy sauce

To make the spring rolls, cut the tuna into pieces 2cm wide and 10cm long. Spread each piece of tuna very lightly with the wasabi paste and roll the tuna in the coriander and parsley. Wrap each piece of tuna in a spring roll wrapper, using a little water to seal the ends.
Deep fry the spring rolls in hot oil for 30–45 seconds or until lightly golden. Drain on absorbent paper. Combine the lime juice and soy and place in small dipping bowls to serve with the tuna rolls and an Asian green salad. Serves 4.

rare tuna spring rolls with lime and soy

eggplant with tomato, basil and parmesan risotto

spiced lamb fillets with onion couscous

chicken baked on sweet potato rosti

white wine risotto with field mushrooms

eggplant with tomato, basil and parmesan risotto

2 small young eggplants (aubergines)
olive oil
risotto
2½ cups (20 fl oz) vegetable or chicken stock
2 cups (16 fl oz) tomato purée
1 cup (8 fl oz) quality red wine
1 tablespoon oil
2 cups arborio rice*
⅓ cup shredded basil
⅓ cup grated parmesan cheese
cracked black pepper

To make the risotto, place the stock, tomato purée and wine in a saucepan over medium heat and allow to simmer. Heat oil in a separate saucepan over medium-high heat. Add the rice and cook for 1 minute or until translucent. Add hot stock mixture, 1 cup at a time, stirring after each cup has been added and absorbed into the rice. Continue adding stock until rice is tender and risotto is creamy. While the risotto is cooking, slice the eggplants and brush well with oil. Place in a preheated frying pan over high heat and cook for 2 minutes on each side or until they are golden; keep warm.
To serve, stir the basil, parmesan and pepper into risotto. Place the eggplant slices onto serving plates and top with the risotto. Serve with a spoonful of creamy goats curd or mascarpone on the side. Serves 4.

chicken baked on sweet potato rosti

4 chicken breast fillets, skin on
sea salt and pepper
sweet potato rosti
550g (1 lb 2 oz) orange sweet potatoes, peeled
2 tablespoons oil
1 clove garlic, crushed
½ cup parmesan cheese
cracked black pepper

Preheat the oven to 220°C (425°F). To make the sweet potato rosti, cut the sweet potato into thin strips using a sharp vegetable peeler. Toss the sweet potato with oil, garlic, parmesan and pepper, and place on a baking tray that is lined with nonstick baking paper. Bake in the oven for 15 minutes.
While sweet potato is cooking, rub salt and pepper into the skin of the chicken. Heat a frying pan over high heat and cook, skin-side down, for 4 minutes. Turn and cook for another minute. Place the chicken on top of the rosti and bake for a further 5 minutes or until chicken is cooked and the sweet potato rosti is crisp and golden brown. Serve with steamed greens. Serves 4.

spiced lamb fillets with onion couscous

1 cup couscous
1¼ cups (10 fl oz) boiling vegetable or chicken stock
2 tablespoons oil
2 onions, sliced
1 tablespoon thyme leaves
spiced lamb
1 tablespoon ground cumin
1 teaspoon ground chilli
1 tablespoon paprika
500g (1 lb) lamb fillets, trimmed
1 tablespoon oil, extra

To make the onion couscous, place couscous and boiling stock in a bowl, cover with plastic wrap and stand for 5 minutes or until all liquid is absorbed. Heat oil in a frying pan over medium heat. Add the onion and thyme and cook for 5–7 minutes or until onion is well browned. Combine the cumin, chilli and paprika and toss with the lamb fillets to coat. Heat another pan with the extra oil over medium-high heat. Add the lamb to pan and cook for 1½–2 minutes on each side or to your liking. Place the couscous in pan with onions and warm through. Slice the lamb and serve with couscous and rocket (arugula) leaves. Serves 4.

white wine risotto with field mushrooms

4 large field mushrooms
oil
cracked black pepper
white wine risotto
4 cups (32 fl oz) vegetable or chicken stock
1½ cups (12 fl oz) quality white wine
2 tablespoons oil
1 leek, chopped
2 cups arborio rice*
3 tablespoons lemon juice
⅓ cup shredded basil
½ cup grated parmesan cheese

To make risotto, place stock and wine in a saucepan over medium heat and allow to simmer rapidly.
Place the oil in a separate saucepan over medium heat. Add the leek and rice and cook for 2 minutes. Add the stock mixture, a few cups at a time, stirring frequently until the stock has been absorbed. Continue adding stock and stirring until all stock is used and rice is al dente and creamy. While risotto is cooking, brush mushrooms with oil and sprinkle with pepper. Place under a preheated hot grill and cook for 5 minutes or until soft. To serve, stir the lemon juice, basil and parmesan through the risotto and place in serving bowls. Top with a mushroom and serve. Serves 4.

spinach and ricotta pies

250g (8 oz) baby English spinach leaves
300g (10 oz) ricotta cheese
1 egg
1/4 cup grated parmesan cheese
2 tablespoons chopped dill
cracked black pepper
2 sheets ready-rolled puff pastry

Preheat oven to 220°C (425°F). Place the spinach into
a saucepan of boiling water for 5 seconds, drain and run
under cold water. Squeeze away any excess liquid and
roughly chop the spinach. Mix the spinach with ricotta,
egg, parmesan, dill and pepper.
Cut each pastry sheet in half. Place the filling on one half
of each piece and fold over, pressing the edges together
to enclose the filling.
Place on a lined baking tray and bake for 15 minutes or
until puffed and golden. Serve with a leaf salad. Serves 4.
note – serve with the roast tomato salad on page 134 of
the short top + sides chapter.

pumpkin and fetta risotto

500g (1 lb) sweet pumpkin, peeled and chopped
oil
sea salt and pepper
fetta risotto
5 1/2 cups (44 fl oz) chicken or vegetable stock
1 tablespoon oil
2 cups arborio rice*
1/4 cup chopped chives
1/4 cup grated parmesan cheese
cracked black pepper
150g (5 oz) marinated fetta in oil

Preheat the oven to 220°C (425°F). Place the pumpkin on
a baking tray and toss with oil, salt and pepper. Bake for
20 minutes or until soft.
To cook the risotto, place stock in a saucepan over medium
heat and allow to simmer. Place oil in a separate saucepan
over medium heat. Add the rice and cook for 1 minute or
until rice is translucent. Add the stock, 1 cup at a time, and
stir until stock has been absorbed. Continue adding until all
the stock has been used, and rice is creamy.
To serve, stir the chives, parmesan, pepper and pumpkin
through risotto. Top with fetta and its oil and serve. Serves 4.
note – serve with the iceberg salad on page 134 of
the short top + sides chapter.

chicken baked in olives, lemon and capers

200g (6 1/2 oz) cherry tomatoes, halved
1/3 cup small lingurian olives
2 teaspoons grated lemon rind
2 tablespoons salted capers, rinsed
2 tablespoons olive oil
cracked black pepper and salt
2 chicken breast fillets

Preheat the oven to 220°C (425°F). Combine the cherry
tomatoes, olives, lemon rind, capers, oil, pepper and salt
and place in the base of a baking dish.
Top with the chicken and spoon a little of the olive mixture
over it to coat. Place in oven and bake, turning the chicken
once, for 20 minutes or until the chicken is cooked.
Serve with boiled potatoes with butter and salt or greens.
Serves 2.

crispy skin rainbow trout with celeriac mash

2 tablespoons sea salt flakes
2 teaspoons cracked black pepper
2 teaspoons juniper berries*, finely chopped
2 tablespoons oil
4 small rainbow (river) trout, gutted and scaled
celeriac mash
3 boiling potatoes, peeled and chopped
1 x 250g (8 oz) celeriac, peeled and chopped
milk
60g (2 oz) butter
sea salt

To make the celeriac mash, place potatoes and celeriac
in a saucepan and cover with milk. Place the saucepan
over medium-high heat and allow to boil gently for
8 minutes or until the potatoes and celeriac are soft.
While the mash is cooking, combine the sea salt flakes,
pepper and juniper berries and rub into the skin of the
trout. Heat the oil in a frying pan over high heat. Add the
fish and cook for 4–5 minutes on each side or until the
skin is crisp and the flesh is tender.
To finish the mash, strain and reserve the hot milk. Add
the butter and salt to the vegetables and mash with some
of the cooking milk until smooth.
Place the mash onto serving plates and top with the trout.
Serve with lemon wedges and a simple side salad of
greens. Serves 4.

spinach and ricotta pies

pumpkin and fetta risotto

chicken baked in olives, lemon and capers

crispy skin rainbow trout with celeriac mash

95

seared scallops on lemon and spinach risotto

double-cooked pork ribs

pork steaks with brown sugar apples

seared scallops on lemon and spinach risotto

1 tablespoon oil
cracked black pepper and sea salt
16 scallops, removed from the shell
lemon and spinach risotto
5½ cups (44 fl oz) vegetable stock
2 tablespoons oil
2 cups arborio rice*
2 teaspoons lemon rind, grated
200g (6½ oz) baby English spinach leaves
cracked black pepper and sea salt
parmesan shavings

To cook the lemon and spinach risotto, place the stock in a saucepan over medium-high heat and allow to come to the boil then reduce to a simmer.
Heat the oil in another saucepan over medium-high heat. Add the rice and cook for 1 minute. Add the stock, 2 cups at a time, stirring frequently and cooking until the stock has been absorbed. Continue adding cups of stock and stirring until all the stock has been absorbed and the rice is tender. Season with pepper and sea salt and keep risotto warm. Heat the oil in a frying pan over high heat. Sprinkle pepper and sea salt over the scallops. Place scallops in the pan and cook for 20–30 seconds on each side or until seared. To serve, stir the lemon rind and the spinach through the risotto and spoon onto serving plates. Top with the scallops and serve with lemon wedges and parmesan on the side. Serves 4.

double-cooked pork ribs

8 pork spare ribs, halved
2 tablespoons soy sauce
3 tablespoons hoisin sauce*
1 tablespoon chilli sauce
1 tablespoon brown sugar

Preheat the oven to 220°C (425°F). Place the pork ribs in the base of a bamboo steamer and steam over a saucepan of boiling water for 6 minutes.
While the ribs are steaming, combine the soy, hoisin, chilli and sugar. Place the ribs on a rack with a baking tray underneath and brush both sides with the sauce. Place in the oven and bake for 10 minutes. Brush the ribs with more sauce, turn and bake for a further 10 minutes. Serve the ribs with steamed greens. Serves 4.
note – for an easy greens with oyster sauce recipe, see page 134 of the short top + sides chapter.

pork steaks with brown sugar apples

4 pork steaks, 1–2cm (½ to ¾ inch) thick
2 tablespoons olive oil
2 tablespoons balsamic vinegar
2 tablespoons chopped sage
brown sugar apples
2 small sweet red apples, sliced
⅓ cup brown sugar
1 tablespoon butter

Place the pork in a shallow dish with the oil, vinegar and sage and set aside.
To make the brown sugar apples, press the apple slices into the brown sugar. Heat a large frying pan over medium-high heat. Add butter and apple slices and cook for 2–3 minutes on each side or until golden and soft; keep warm.
Heat a frying pan over high heat. Add the pork to pan without the marinade and cook for 3–5 minutes on each side or to your liking. Serve the pork with the brown sugar apples and steamed green vegetables. Serves 4.

corn cakes with prosciutto salad

2 cobs corn
1 cup self-raising (self-rising) flour
2 eggs
¼ cup coriander, shredded
1 teaspoon ground cumin
1 teaspoon baking powder (baking soda)
pinch sea salt
prosciutto salad
125g (4 oz) baby English spinach or rocket (arugula) leaves
½ cup semi-dried tomatoes, with oil
12 slices prosciutto*
cracked black pepper

Place the corn in a saucepan of boiling water and cook until tender. Remove corn kernels from the cob. Place the flour, eggs, coriander, cumin, baking powder and salt into a food processor and process until combined. Add the corn and process until corn is roughly chopped.
Spread 2–3 tablespoons of mixture into a hot, greased frying pan and cook for 3 minutes on each side or until golden. Keep warm and repeat with remaining mixture.
To serve, place a corn cake on each serving plate and top with the spinach or rocket, semi-dried tomatoes, prosciutto and pepper. Drizzle over the oil from the semi-dried tomatoes and top with another corn cake. Serve immediately. Serves 4.

corn cakes with prosciutto salad

soft polenta with blue cheese and wine beef

2 cups (16 fl oz) hot water
2 cups (16 fl oz) milk
1 cup instant-cooking polenta
60g (2 oz) butter
cracked black pepper and sea salt
150g (5 oz) soft, strong blue cheese
wine beef
1 tablespoon oil
4 fillet steaks
¾ cup (6 fl oz) red wine
¾ cup (6 fl oz) beef stock

Place the water and milk in a saucepan and bring to the boil. Remove from heat and slowly whisk in the polenta. Return to low heat and stir for 3 minutes or until polenta is soft and creamy. Add the butter and pepper and salt, stir through and keep warm.
To make the wine beef, heat the oil in a frying pan over medium-high heat. Add the steaks and cook for 3–4 minutes on each side or until cooked to your liking. Remove from the pan, cover and keep warm. Add the wine and stock to the pan and boil until reduced by half. To serve, place a large spoonful of polenta onto the serving plates and top with the blue cheese. Serve with the steak and the pan juices as the sauce. Serves 4.

thai chicken salad

1 tablespoon oil
1 tablespoon chopped ginger
1 stalk lemongrass*, chopped
3 red chillies, chopped
500g (1 lb) minced chicken breast
¼ cup (2 fl oz) lemon juice
1 tablespoon fish sauce*
1 red onion, thinly sliced
1 cup coriander leaves
2 tablespoons shredded basil
lettuce leaves to serve

Heat the oil in a frying pan over high heat. Add the ginger, lemongrass and chilli and cook for 1 minute. Then add the chicken and cook, stirring to break up any lumps, for 5 minutes or until the chicken is cooked.
Remove the chicken from heat and cool slightly. Combine the lemon juice and fish sauce, and pour it over the chicken. Add the onion, coriander and basil. Serve the salad in small bowls with side plates of crisp lettuce leaves to eat with the salad. Serves 4.

salmon baked in salsa verde

4 x 150g (5 oz) pieces salmon fillet
salsa verde
⅓ cup chopped dill
⅓ cup flat-leaf (Italian) parsley, chopped
⅓ cup mint, chopped
2 cloves garlic, sliced
1 tablespoon dijon mustard
8 anchovy fillets
3 tablespoons salted capers, rinsed
⅓ cup (2¾ fl oz) olive oil
2 tablespoons lemon juice

Preheat the oven to 200°C (400°F). To make the salsa verde, place the dill, parsley, mint, garlic, mustard, anchovies and capers into a food processor and process until smooth. Then add the olive oil and lemon juice and process until combined.
Place the salmon in a baking dish and spread with the salsa verde. Bake for 6–10 minutes or until the salmon is cooked medium-rare. Serve with steamed greens. Serves 4.

lamb rack with preserved lemon gremolata crust

500g (1 lb) baby new potatoes
sea salt
olive oil
1 lamb rack of 12 cutlets
preserved lemon gremolata
2 cloves garlic, crushed
⅔ cup flat-leaf (Italian) parsley, chopped
1½ tablespoons chopped preserved lemon rind*
2 tablespoons olive oil

Preheat the oven to 220°C (425°F). Place the potatoes in a baking dish with sea salt and olive oil and shake to coat. Place in oven and bake for 15 minutes.
Remove the excess fat from the lamb. Heat a frying pan over high heat then add the lamb and cook for 3 minutes or until meat is sealed. Remove from pan and set aside. To make the preserved lemon gremolata, combine the garlic, parsley, preserved lemon rind and oil. Spread the gremolata over the lamb and then place in the baking dish with the potatoes. Bake for 12–15 minutes or until lamb is cooked to your liking. To serve, place potatoes on serving plates. Slice rack into cutlets and serve with steamed greens. Serves 4.
note – you may need to shield the gremolata from the heat with a little strip of aluminium foil to prevent it from burning, depending on how long you cook the lamb for.

soft polenta with blue cheese and wine beef

salmon baked in salsa verde

thai chicken salad

lamb rack with preserved lemon gremolata crust

steamed lemongrass chicken and rice rolls

steamed lemongrass chicken and rice rolls

4 stalks lemongrass*, halved lengthwise
3 chicken breast fillets, halved lengthwise
1 tablespoon sesame oil
2 red chillies, seeded and chopped
1 bunch gai larn (Chinese broccoli), halved
300g (10 oz) plain rice-noodle rolls*
soy sauce to serve

Place the lemongrass in the base of a bamboo steamer.
Top with the chicken and then brush the chicken with
the sesame oil and sprinkle with chilli. Place a lid on the
steamer and then place it over a saucepan of boiling water
and steam for 3 minutes.
While the chicken is steaming, place the gai larn and rice
rolls in another bamboo steamer of the same size. Place the
noodle steamer on top of the steamer with the chicken and
cover. Steam for a further 5 minutes or until chicken and gai
larn are tender. Serve with small bowls of soy sauce and
wedges of lime. Serves 4.

tempura fish with chilli salad

1 quantity tempura batter (see page 165 of basics chapter)
2 small fish such as snapper or coral trout, gutted and scaled
flour to coat
oil for frying
chilli salad
2 large, mild red chillies, seeded and sliced
1/2 Lebanese cucumber, shredded
1/2 red onion, sliced
2 tablespoons chopped coriander
2 tablespoons chopped mint
1 tablespoon lemon juice
1 tablespoon soy sauce

To make the chilli salad, combine the chilli, cucumber,
onion, coriander, mint, lemon and soy, and set aside.
To make the tempura fish, coat the fish lightly in flour and
shake away excess. Dip the fish into the batter and place
into a wok of hot oil over high or medium-high heat. Cook
for 5 minutes on each side or until golden and crisp. Drain
on absorbent paper and serve with the chilli salad. Serves 4.

parmesan polenta with garlic-grilled vegetables

2 cups (16 fl oz) hot water
2 cups (16 fl oz) milk
1 cup instant-cooking polenta
1/3 cup grated parmesan cheese
60g (2 oz) butter
cracked black pepper and sea salt
garlic-grilled vegetables
1/2 cup (4 fl oz) olive oil
3 cloves garlic, chopped
cracked black pepper and salt
2 capsicums, halved
2 zucchinis (courgettes), halved
2 raddichio hearts, halved

Place the water and milk in a saucepan and bring to the
boil. Remove from heat and slowly whisk in the polenta.
Return to heat and stir for 3 minutes or until polenta is soft
and creamy. Add the parmesan, butter and pepper and salt,
stir through and keep warm.
To make the garlic-grilled vegetables, combine the oil, garlic
and pepper and salt. Brush well over the vegetables and
place under a preheated hot grill and cook for 2–3 minutes
on each side or until golden. Serve the vegetables with the
parmesan polenta. Serves 4.

stir fry pork and shiitake

2 teaspoons sesame oil
2 teaspoons oil
2 tablespoons shredded ginger
2 cloves garlic, sliced
500g (1 lb) pork fillet, sliced
cornflour
200g (6 1/2 oz) fresh shiitake mushrooms*
1/2 cup (4 fl oz) Chinese cooking wine* or sherry
3 tablespoons soy sauce
8 baby bok choy, leaves separated

Heat the oils in a wok or frying pan over high heat. Add
the ginger and garlic and cook for 1 minute. Lightly toss the
pork in cornflour and shake away excess. Add the pork to
pan and cook for 4 minutes or until well sealed.
Add the mushrooms, wine, soy and bok choy to pan and
stir fry for 3–4 minutes or until mushrooms and bok choy
are tender. Serve with rice and small bowls of chopped
chilli on the side. Serves 4.

tempura fish with chilli salad

parmesan polenta with garlic-grilled vegetables

stir fry pork and shiitake

chicken poached in ginger broth

5 cups (40 fl oz) chicken stock
2 tablespoons shredded ginger
2 coriander roots
350g (11 oz) sweet potato, peeled and sliced
4 chicken breast fillets, halved lengthwise
3 shallots (green onions), sliced

Place the chicken stock, ginger and coriander roots in a deep frying pan over medium-high heat and allow to rapidly simmer for 2 minutes.
Add the sweet potato to the pan and simmer for 4 minutes.
Add the chicken to pan and simmer for a further 5 minutes or until the chicken and sweet potato are soft and tender.
To serve, place the chicken and sweet potato in serving bowls and spoon over the ginger broth. Sprinkle with shallots and serve. Serves 4.

pizza with tomato, olives and rosemary

1 quantity dough (see page 179 of basics chapter)
or 4 ready-made pizza bases
oil
topping
6 bocconcini*, sliced
300g (10 oz) cherry tomatoes, halved
1/3 cup small olives
1/3 cup caper berries*
2 tablespoons rosemary sprigs
12 slices prosciutto* or coppa
cracked black pepper

Preheat oven to 220°C (425°F). Place two baking trays that will fit the pizzas into the oven to heat. If using fresh dough, divide into 4 pieces and roll out on a lightly floured surface until 2–3mm (1/3 inch) thick.
Place the pizza bases onto nonstick baking paper and brush well with oil. Top with bocconcini, tomatoes, olives, caper berries, rosemary, prosciutto and pepper.
Slide the pizzas on the paper onto the hot baking trays and place in oven. Bake for 15 minutes or until the crust is golden. Serve with salad greens. Serves 4.
note – this recipe can also be baked in a tart shell. Place the topping ingredients in a blind-baked pepper and mustard or parmesan shortcrust pastry shell (see page 173 of basics chapter) and bake for 10–15 minutes.

roast beef with sweet pumpkin

8–12 wedges Jap or sweet pumpkin
3 parsnips, peeled and halved
2 tablespoons oil
sea salt and cracked black pepper
600g (11/4 lb) eye fillet or scotch fillet
1 bunch lemon thyme

Preheat the oven to 220°C (425°F). Place the pumpkin, parsnip, oil, salt and pepper in a baking dish and toss to combine. Place in the oven and bake for 15 minutes while sealing the meat.
Heat a frying pan over high heat. Add the fillet and cook for 1 minute on each side or until well browned and sealed. Place the lemon thyme in the base of the baking dish with the pumpkin and then rest the fillet on top of the lemon thyme. Return to the oven and cook for 15 minutes or until the meat is cooked to your liking and the pumpkin is soft and golden. Serves 4.

steak sandwiches with roast garlic

1 tablespoon oil
1 onion, sliced
8 thick slices tomato
8 thin fillet steaks
8 slices bread, toasted
roast garlic
2 heads garlic, halved
olive oil
sea salt

Preheat the oven to 240°C (475°F). To roast the garlic, place it in a small baking dish and drizzle with oil and salt. Cover and bake for 20 minutes or until the garlic is soft. While the garlic is roasting, heat the oil in a nonstick frying pan over high heat. Add onion and cook for 3–4 minutes or until golden; set aside.
Place tomato slices in pan and cook for 2 minutes on each side or until browned; set aside.
Place the steaks in the hot pan and cook for 1 minute on each side or to your liking. Remove from the pan and return the onion and tomato to the pan to heat.
Place the onion, tomato and steaks on the bread. Spread the remaining slices of bread and the steaks with the roast garlic and serve. Serves 4.

chicken poached in ginger broth

roast beef with sweet pumpkin

pizza with tomato, olives and rosemary

steak sandwiches with roast garlic

blood plum tarts

parmesan shortbreads

sugar-roasted fruit

blood plum tarts

125g (4 oz) butter, softened
1/2 cup caster (superfine) sugar
2 eggs
1 teaspoon vanilla extract
3/4 cup ground almonds
1/3 cup plain (all-purpose) flour
4 blood plums, stones removed

Preheat the oven to 200°C (400°F). Place the butter
and sugar in a food processor and process until smooth.
Add the eggs, vanilla, almonds and flour, and process until
just combined.
Place a plum in each individual ovenproof bowl. Spoon the
almond mixture around the plum and bake in the oven for
15–20 minutes or until filling is puffed and golden. Serves 4.

parmesan shortbreads

125g (4 oz) butter
1 cup plain (all-purpose) flour
1/3 cup grated parmesan cheese
1 teaspoon cracked black pepper

Preheat the oven to 170°C (325°F). Place the butter, flour,
parmesan and pepper into a food processor and process
until a smooth dough forms.
Place tablespoons of shortbread mixture onto baking trays
lined with nonstick baking paper. Bake for 15–20 minutes
or until lightly browned on the base of the shortbread.
Cool on wire racks and serve with cheese and quince paste
after dinner. Makes 16 shortbreads.

sugar-roasted fruit

2 nectarines or peaches, halved
4 plums, halved
2 tablespoons sugar

Preheat the oven to 220°C (425°F). Place the nectarines
or peaches and the plums into a baking dish lined with
nonstick paper. Sprinkle the fruit with sugar and place
in the oven for 20 minutes or until the sugar is golden.
Serve the roasted fruit with thick cream or vanilla-bean
ice cream. Serves 4.

grilled ricotta and muscatel panettone sandwiches

1/3 cup marsala
1/3 cup seedless muscatels or raisins
8 slices panettone
100g (3 1/2 oz) fresh ricotta cheese
icing sugar

Place the marsala in a saucepan over medium heat and
cook until simmering. Add the muscatels, remove the pan
from heat and stand until the marsala has been absorbed
into the muscatels.
Top half of the panettone slices with the muscatels and then
top with the ricotta and another slice of panettone. Sprinkle
the panettone with icing sugar and place on a preheated
grill or grill pan and toast for 1 minute on each side or until
golden. Serve with a good dessert wine or liqueur. Serves 4.
note – serve with the vanilla coffee on page 118 of the
short top + sides chapter.

grilled ricotta and muscatel panettone sandwiches

coconut rice with lime syrup

1 cup long-grain rice
2½ cups (20 fl oz) water
¾ cup coconut cream
2 tablespoons caster (superfine) sugar
lime syrup
¼ cup grated dark palm sugar*
½ cup (4 fl oz) water
¼ cup (2 fl oz) lime juice
1 tablespoon shredded lime rind
chilled coconut cream to serve

Place the rice in a colander and wash well. Place rice and water in a saucepan over medium-high heat and bring to the boil. Allow to simmer rapidly for 10 minutes or until almost all of the water has been absorbed. Add coconut cream and caster sugar, cover saucepan and place over very low heat for 5 minutes.
While the rice is cooking, place the palm sugar, water, juice and rind into a small saucepan over medium-low heat and allow to simmer for 4 minutes or until mixture is syrupy.
To serve, place coconut rice into bowls and spoon over the syrup. Serve with chilled coconut cream. Serves 4–6.

cinnamon-crusted pancakes

1 quantity pancake batter (see page 164 of basics chapter)
½ cup sugar
1 tablespoon ground cinnamon
60g (2 oz) butter, melted

Make the pancake mixture according to basics chapter. Cook 3–4 tablespoons of the mixture in a nonstick frying pan over medium heat until puffed and golden on both sides. Remove pancake from pan, set aside and continue cooking the remaining mixture.
Combine the sugar and cinnamon in a shallow bowl. Brush both sides of the pancake lightly with the melted butter and then press it lightly into the sugar mixture and turn to coat both sides.
Cook the pancake in a nonstick frying pan over high heat for 45 seconds on each side or until the sugar has melted and caramelised. Place on a plate and keep warm.
Serve the pancakes in a small stack with a side bowl of ice cream. Serves 4–6.

coconut chocolate tarts

2 egg whites
½ cup sugar
2 cups desiccated coconut
filling
1¼ cups (10 fl oz) cream
300g (10 oz) quality dark chocolate, chopped

Preheat the oven to 180°C (350°F). Place the egg whites, sugar and coconut in a bowl and mix to combine them. With wetted hands or a spoon, press the coconut mixture into eight, ¾ cup (6 fl oz) capacity, deep muffin tins, covering the base and sides to make a shell. Place in a preheated oven and bake for 8–10 minutes or until the shells are just beginning to turn a light golden colour. Cool the shells for 1 minute then gently remove them from the tin and place on a wire rack.
Make the filling while the bases are cooking. Place the cream in a saucepan over medium heat and heat until almost boiling. Remove the cream from heat. Add the chopped chocolate and stir through until the chocolate has melted and the filling is smooth.
Pour the chocolate filling into the coconut tart shells and place in the freezer for 10 minutes or until the chocolate filling is set. Serve with coffee or berries as a dessert. Makes 8 tarts.

little passionfruit cheesecakes

4 shortbread biscuits
topping
250g (8 oz) ricotta cheese
250g (8 oz) cream cheese, chopped
2 eggs
½ cup sugar
2 tablespoons lime juice
⅔ cup fresh passionfruit pulp

Preheat the oven to 160°C (315°F). Place one shortbread biscuit in the base of 4 ramekins. Place the ricotta, cream cheese, eggs, sugar and lime juice in a food processor and process until the mixture is smooth.
Stir through the passionfruit pulp and then spoon the mixture into each ramekin. Bake in the oven for 15 minutes or until the topping is firm. Serve warm or cold. Serves 4.

coconut rice with lime syrup

coconut chocolate tarts

cinnamon-crusted pancakes

little passionfruit cheesecakes

hort
top +
sides

morning

breakfast sandwich   milky porridge with berries

grilled sugar cinnamon doughnuts

morning

breakfast sandwich

of crispy bacon, grilled sliced tomato, baby English spinach leaves and aged cheddar. Place it all between toasted bread with substance such as sourdough or grain bread. Wrap in napkins and serve in the lounge room or on the balcony soaking up the morning sun with two newspapers, fresh juices and coffee.

milky porridge

with berries to turn winter on its head. Top piping hot milky oat porridge with frozen blueberries and raspberries—easily found in the supermarket freezer—and then sprinkle with brown sugar and pour a milk float around the sides of the bowl. The berries will thaw in the hot porridge in no time, making the porridge the right temperature to tuck right into.

grilled sugar

cinnamon doughnuts are a very urban breakfast. Place ready-made sugar and cinnamon coated doughnuts in a grill pan and top with a plate to weight them down. Cook for 2 minutes on each side or until sugar has caramelised and the doughnut is toasted and crisp. Have this with a good strong coffee before a hard day ahead.

melon and coconut

frappés are the perfect way to stay cooled on a hot summer morning. Blend chopped honeydew melon or rockmelon with a few sprigs of mint, a dollop of coconut cream and lots of ice until smooth then pour into big, tall glasses for a summer morning pick up and chill out.

baked eggs

are simple and delicious. Line a few small bowls with blanched baby English spinach and sprinkle with sea salt and cracked black pepper. Break an egg into the centre of the spinach and bake in a preheated 180°C (350°F) oven for 12–16 minutes, depending on how you like the yolk cooked. Serve with hot buttered toast. You can also place sautéed mushrooms or slices of aged cheddar in the bowl with the spinach.

soaked bircher

muesli is simple if you are a little more organised than most. Make a batch of bircher muesli by placing 2 cups of quality muesli packed with grains, fruit and nuts in a bowl. Pour 1 cup (8 fl oz) of cream and 1 cup (8 fl oz) of milk over it and refrigerate overnight. Serve with sliced fresh fruit and extra milk.

toasted pistachio

and honey yoghurt is a perfect combination. Try thick, sweet honey poured into the base of small cups or bowls, sprinkled with roughly chopped toasted fresh pistachio nuts and then topped off with lots of creamy thick yoghurt. Run your spoon down the side of the glass or bowl to the bottom and then drag it through the honey, nuts and yoghurt to get all three flavours.

vanilla coffee

pure vanilla extract delivers a hint of mellow flavour to a good strong coffee. Place a drop or two of good-quality vanilla extract in your morning coffee before adding milk. For a real kick, add a generous teaspoon of vanilla to a strong short black—great for after dinner. Pure vanilla extract that is thick and pungent has the best flavour.

rhubarb and ricotta

on toasted warm raisin and cinnamon bread. Spread the toast with thick and creamy fresh ricotta. Top this with short lengths of rhubarb that have been simmered in orange juice until soft. Drizzle the whole lot lightly with honey or pure maple syrup. Eat fairly quickly so that the crisp toast doesn't sog.

melon and coconut frappés   baked eggs

soaked bircher muesli

toasted pistachio and honey yoghurt

vanilla coffee   rhubarb and ricotta toast

lunchbox

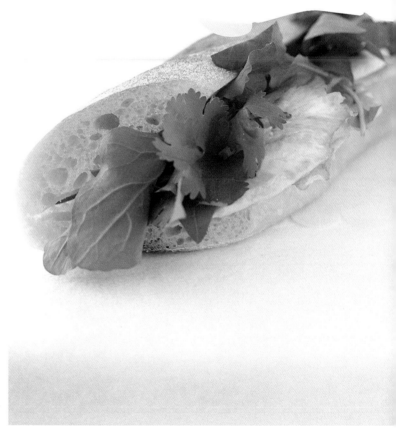

little frittatas

thai herb and chicken baguette

lunchbox pies

lunchbox

little frittatas

served hot or cold are great to serve at a picnic or portable occasion. A good base mixture is 6 eggs, 1½ cups (12 fl oz) cream and cracked black pepper. To this, add good things such as crispy bacon, parsley, grated quality cheddar, pesto, roast pumpkin or potato pieces. Pour mixture into deep nonstick muffin tins and bake at 180°C (350°F) for 20–30 minutes or until the frittatas are firm.

thai herb

and chicken baguette is a new take on the chicken and mayo sandwich. Zingy Thai herbs such as Thai basil, mint and coriander packed in sourdough baguettes with sliced grilled chicken and whole-egg mayonnaise mixed with lemon juice and cracked black pepper.

lunchbox pies

Cut rounds of puff pastry and top with cooked chicken and roasted sweet potato or sliced roast lamb and chutney. Cut larger rounds of pastry to cover. Seal the edges, place them on a baking tray and bake at 200°C (400°F) for 20 minutes or until puffed and golden. Serve warm or cold in lunchboxes with a fizzy drink or a rich-flavoured milk to wash them down.

chilli bean

tortilla sandwiches make a crisp snack with punch. Combine your favourite beans with chilli sauce and spread over a tortilla. Sprinkle with grated cheese and top with another tortilla. Place in a greased frying pan with a plate and a weight (such as a large can) on top and cook until crisp. Flip the tortilla and repeat until both sides are crisp and filling is heated through.

simple tomato

sandwich of ripe, red tomato slices, your favourite cheese, torn basil leaves, sea salt and cracked black pepper. We like a sandwich when there are only two decisions to make—which bread and which cheese.

grilled lime

and chilli chicken teamed with chilled champagne. Cook the chicken pieces that have been marinating in chilli and lime juice under a hot grill until tender and well browned. Place into boxes with lots of napkins and well-chilled tiny bottles of French champagne. You'll be the envy of the picnic!

chocolate

cup cakes replace mung bean rolls, tofu sandwiches and banana soya drink. Fill your lunchbox with chocolate cupcakes, lollies and chocolates. Go on, you can do it and your friends will love you for it. Use the little chocolate brownies recipe on page 78 of the 20 minute chapter and cook them in patty cases.

risotto cakes

are easily made from leftovers of your favourite flavoured risotto. Make the cooled risotto into a flat patty in your hand. Place a piece of bocconcini or marinated fetta in the middle and squash the risotto over the cheese to enclose. Shallow fry the risotto cakes in hot oil until golden and crisp then drain on absorbent paper. Serve with a simple leaf salad or make small cakes to go with drinks.

sticky banana

rice packed and rolled in paper makes this treat ready to go anywhere. Cook long-grain rice in the usual absorption method. Add ⅓ cup coconut cream and sugar to taste, cover and stand the hot rice for 4 minutes. Spread the rice along nonstick paper or banana leaves to form a flat rectangle. Place some finely chopped banana or mango down the centre and top with more rice to enclose the fruit. Roll up the paper or banana leaf.

chilli bean tortilla sandwiches

simple tomato sandwich

grilled lime and chilli chicken

risotto cakes

chocolate cup cakes

sticky banana rice

quick bite

garlic bruschetta

chilli popcorn

the wedge of cheese

quick bite

garlic bruschetta

made with a good wood-fired loaf of bread drizzled with olive oil, grilled until golden and crisp and then rubbed with a clove of garlic or a handful of basil. Top with thin slices of ripe tomato and slices of olive, goats curd or a salad of shredded rocket (arugula), red onion and capers. Great served any time.

chilli popcorn

is great for couch video days or to accompany a cold beer. Pop some popping corn in a hot frying pan and toss with butter, sea salt and chilli powder while the popcorn is still hot. Great when there are lots of peckish people about, as you can make a huge bowl in just minutes.

the wedge

of cheese. Only one cheese means the flavours don't blend or clash and if it's a great cheese, it should stand alone to make a simple supper. Whether it is a big gutsy blue or a ripe and runny Brie, purchase the best quality cheese you can find. Serve simple accompaniments such as oatcakes, wafers, dried Persian figs or sundried pears. Serve a suitably matched wine—blue cheese is great with a sticky botrytis affected riesling and Brie with a peppery young pinot noir.

jaffles

break out the jaffle (toasted sandwich) maker for a quick snack. Cheeses such as Gruyère and cheddar, leftover roast chicken or roast lamb with onion marmalade, a whole egg (for the machines without the cut-in-half action) with double smoked ham and mustard, and a quick confession for Sunday afternoon—smoked ham, cheddar and pineapple.

steamed pork

buns are a snap when purchased from the freezer section in Asian supermarkets. Steam them straight from the freezer for 10–15 minutes over rapidly boiling water and serve with hot chilli sauce. Often labelled as cha sui buns, or barbecue pork buns. Try the different brands to find a good one.

goats curd

flavoured with a little good fruity olive oil and a squeeze of lemon could be that special something you're looking for to go with that Sunday afternoon glass of red. Serve with warm bread or crackers.

spiced ricotta

and grilled figs can be made by mixing ground cinnamon and freshly grated nutmeg through fresh creamy ricotta. Sweeten the ricotta with a little sugar and spread over thickly sliced and toasted fruit bread. Top all this with sliced figs and sprinkle with brown sugar. Place under a hot grill and cook until the sugar has caramelised and figs are warm.

hot smoked

salmon salad of crunchy mixed lettuce leaves and sprigs of chervil piled high on serving plates. Break the salmon into large chunks, straight from the fillet. Top with a simple lemon and oil vinaigrette and serve with slices of tangy sourdough bread.

coconut

macaroons are a simple one-bowl no-fuss cookie. Use the coconut base recipe for the coconut chocolate tarts on page 112. With wetted hands, press large tablespoons of the mixture into balls and place on a lined baking tray. Flatten the coconut balls slightly and place in a preheated 180°C (350°F) oven and bake for 10–15 minutes or until the base is golden. Serve with coffee or hot chocolate.

jaffles

steamed pork buns

goats curd

spiced ricotta and grilled figs

hot smoked salmon salad

coconut macaroons

evening

macaroni cheese

kitchen sink omelette

graze platter

evening

macaroni cheese

is perfect comfort food. Cook a couple of handfuls of macaroni in boiling water until tender, drain and return to the saucepan with a little cream or milk, mustard and cracked black pepper. Stir for 2 minutes over low heat then stir through some chopped flat-leaf (Italian) parsley and place in ovenproof dishes. Top with grated cheese and lots of cracked black pepper. Bake until cheese has melted and is golden brown.

kitchen sink

omelette—my Dad's special for Sunday night. Take almost anything from the fridge that looks like a leftover—roast potatoes, pumpkin, roast lamb, cheese, tomatoes, whatever. Place them in a frying pan over medium heat and cook until warm. Beat eggs and season with salt and pepper. Pour over the vegetables and stir to let the egg get to the bottom of the pan. Cook over low heat until almost set then grill the top. Cut into chunks and serve with hot buttered toast.

graze platter

of tasty morsels makes for a perfect relaxed dinner. A wedge of baked ricotta, paper-thin pancetta or prosciutto, tomato salad with basil and red onion, hommus or baba ghanoush, marinated olives and slices of good-quality bread. Team all this with a glass of good red to complete the story.

duck pancakes

are easy when you cheat a little and purchase a Chinese barbecue duck from a good Chinese barbecue shop and ask them to chop it for you. While you are at the barbecue shop or near an Asian grocer, pick up some Peking pancakes from the freezer section or purchase them warm from a Chinese barbecue shop. Serve the duck warm with the warm pancakes, chopped shallots (green onions) and hoisin sauce.

ravioli

on baby spinach makes dinner in a snap. Place baby English spinach or rocket (arugula) leaves in the bottom of pasta bowls. Drop good-quality fresh ravioli in plenty of boiling water and cook until tender. Drain and place on the spinach or rocket leaves and top with a piece of butter, cracked black pepper and parmesan.

crisp potato

cakes with salmon—simple and delicious. Grate 2 large potatoes into a bowl and mix with 2 tablespoons of melted butter and 1 tablespoon of chopped dill or parsley. Cook flattened spoonfuls of this mixture in an oiled pan until crisp and golden. Pile onto plates and top with smoked salmon or trout, watercress or similar greens and crème fraîche.

chilli, garlic

and lemon spaghetti that is easy and will fill a hungry stomach is only minutes away. Just place some pasta in a large saucepan of boiling water to cook. Place a couple of tablespoons of fruity olive oil, chopped chilli, sliced garlic and some grated lemon rind in a frying pan and cook until fragrant. Toss with the cooked pasta. Anchovies, pepper and parmesan are optional.

steak sandwich

with brown onion rings and a spicy mustard is one of those things I sometimes get a craving for. Toast thick slices of bread until golden. Place a few pieces of eye or scotch fillet into a very hot frying pan with a few onion rings and cook until steak is cooked to your liking and the onion is golden and crisp. Place on the toasted bread with grain mustard and salad greens. Serve with crunchy potato chips if you are really hungry.

cheat's sushi

is easy—make the sushi rice using 1 cup of short-grain rice and 2½ cups (20 fl oz) of water. Cook over high heat until tunnels form in the rice then remove from heat and cover tightly for 5 minutes. Place in a glass or ceramic bowl and stir through 3 tablespoons of rice vinegar and a little sea salt. Cut nori sheets into squares and top with some of the rice and your favourite sashimi slices. Serve with soy sauce and ginger.

duck pancakes

ravioli on baby spinach

crisp potato cakes with salmon

chilli, garlic and lemon spaghetti

steak sandwich

cheat's sushi

sides

asparagus with balsamic butter   roast garlic mash

warm walnut dressing over rocket

sides

asparagus

with balsamic butter makes the perfect side to many dishes. Simply melt a generous amount of butter in a frying pan over medium heat. Then add some balsamic vinegar and a couple of bunches of trimmed asparagus. Cook until the asparagus is tender and serve with parmesan cheese and cracked black pepper.

roast garlic

mash potatoes with cream and butter. Place a halved head of garlic in the oven. Sprinkle with olive oil and roast for about 30 minutes or until golden and soft—squeeze the soft garlic from the skins. Boil peeled and chopped potatoes until soft—look for the varieties labelled good for mashing. Mash the potatoes with butter, sea salt, cream and most of the roast garlic. Top with more sea salt, melted butter and the last of the roast garlic. For a smooth creamy mash, press the potatoes through a 'mouli' food mill. This is a comforting warm side for just about anything.

warm walnut dressing

over rocket (arugula) leaves. Place a good splash or two of olive oil in a small saucepan and add a big handful of walnuts and a few sprigs of rosemary leaves. Heat over low heat to infuse the flavours through the oil. Pour over the rocket (arugula) leaves and finish with a squeeze of lemon juice, cracked black pepper and olives. Serve immediately before the rocket wilts.

roast tomato

salad piled with torn basil leaves. Halve the tomatoes and place, flesh-side up, in a baking dish. Sprinkle with a little olive oil and pepper and bake in a preheated 200°C (400°F) oven until soft. Serve warm or cold with a big bunch of roughly shredded young basil leaves, balsamic vinegar, olive oil and more pepper. Shave parmesan cheese over the top before serving.

greens

with oyster sauce is an easy way to eat your greens. Fry up a few tablespoons of shredded ginger in some sesame oil. Add ¼ cup (2 fl oz) oyster sauce, ¼ cup (2 fl oz) Chinese cooking wine or dry sherry, ¼ cup (2 fl oz) salt-reduced soy and allow to simmer. Add brown sugar to taste. Blanch some Asian greens such as bok choy, choy sum or gai larn in boiling water for 10–20 seconds. Drain and then place on a serving plate. Top with the sauce and serve.

salt and rosemary

baked potatoes are the perfect side to serve with almost anything. Generous amounts of sea salt, olive oil and rosemary sprigs tossed with baby new potatoes. Bake in a hot oven, shaking the pan once while cooking, until potatoes are soft and golden.

pine nut

butter with beans is a perfect combination. Place 80g (2¾ oz) butter in a saucepan and add a couple of tablespoons of chopped pine nuts. Cook over low heat until the butter and pine nuts are golden then add 2–3 tablespoons of lemon juice. Pour the browned butter over steamed green beans, wilted spinach, blanched broccoli etc. Top with cracked black pepper and serve.

iceberg

salad is simple and easy. Remove the outer leaves from a crisp iceberg lettuce. Halve the lettuce crosswise so you have a section of halved lettuce cups. Make a simple dressing of even quantities of oil and vinegar mixed with mustard, fresh herbs, sea salt and cracked black pepper. Pour dressing over lettuce and serve. Before you start, if your lettuce is not as crisp as it should be, soak it in a large bowl of iced water to refresh.

sesame sweet

potato. Brush the peeled long sweet potato slices with combined vegetable and sesame oil. Sprinkle with sea salt and place in a 200°C (400°F) oven and bake until the sweet potato is golden. Serve as a hot vegetable side or cool and serve with salad greens and a simple dressing.

roast tomato salad   greens with oyster sauce

salt and rosemary baked potatoes   pine nut butter with beans

iceberg salad   sesame sweet potato

sweet fix

ice cream with chocolate sticks   panna cotta

really real hot chocolate

sweet fix

ice cream

with chocolate sticks is a great way to be a big kid. Pile up scoops of your favourite, flavoured good-quality ice cream. Serve with chocolate-covered stick biscuits to be used as the spoon. The spoon often accidentally gets eaten so have a pile of them on hand.

panna cotta

is easy to make en masse for large gatherings of friends. Place 1 split vanilla bean, ¾ cup icing sugar, 2 cups (16 fl oz) cream and 1 cup (8 fl oz) milk into a saucepan over medium heat and bring almost to the boil. Soak 1 tablespoon of gelatine in 3 tablespoons of cold water. Whisk gelatine into cream mixture, allow to just bubble for 4 minutes. Pour into ramekins or Chinese tea cups and refrigerate for 4–6 hours or until set. Serve with mixed berries in summer or wedges of sugar-grilled ruby grapefruit in winter.

really real hot chocolate

is the best and is made by placing chopped dark chocolate in the bottom of a tall glass. Pour in heated milk to almost fill the glass. Stir to melt the chocolate into the milk. Serve with extra chocolate on the side to nibble on—oooohhhh.

rice pudding

made in small bowls or ramekins is fast and easy. Place 1–2 tablespoons of cooked rice in the bottom of each bowl. Top with a mixture of 4 eggs, ½ cup sugar, 2½ cups (20 fl oz) milk and 1 teaspoon vanilla extract that has been whisked together. Place the bowls in a baking dish and half-fill the dish with hot water. Sprinkle with cinnamon or freshly grated nutmeg and bake in a preheated 160°C (315°F) oven for 20–25 minutes or until puddings are just set. Remove from baking dish and eat warm or cold.

a chocolate wedge

of melt-in-your-mouth, drop-dead-delicious, couverture chocolate. Place it on a sturdy platter or board in the middle of the table. Serve with utensils for breaking the chocolate such as an ice pick or knife. Accompany with a glass of torquay, liqueur muscat or port.

ice cream sandwiches

make ice cream sandwiches using good-quality shortbread or chocolate-coated biscuits and your choice of ice cream. Sandwich between biscuits and refreeze for 5–10 minutes or until firm.

raspberry yoghurt

ice cream is a creamy ice delight with zing. Place 1kg (2 lb) thick plain yoghurt, 300g (10 oz) frozen raspberries, ¼ cup (2 fl oz) lemon or lime juice and 1 cup of sugar in the bowl of an ice cream machine and churn until frozen raspberry yoghurt appears—serve with crispy wafers. Store any leftovers in a covered metal container in the freezer.

caramel pears

with pancakes will hit the spot on a cold afternoon or evening. Make pancakes from the batter on page 164 of the basics chapter. Cook some pear slices in 60g (2 oz) butter and 3 tablespoons brown sugar until soft. Layer the pears between the pancakes in a stack. Add an extra 3 tablespoons of brown sugar to the pan with 1 cup (8 fl oz) cream. Allow to slowly simmer until it is a thick caramel sauce. Pour over the pancake stack and serve.

quince jelly

on scones either made by you if you are feeling energetic or purchased from your favourite cake or pastry shop. Place the scones, covered in a tea towel, in a warm oven if you have to reheat them. Serve with quince jelly or homemade strawberry jam—often found at street cake sales or fêtes and sold by older ladies wearing aprons of envy. Serve with thick cream or sweetened whipped cream on the side.

rice pudding

a chocolate wedge

ice cream sandwiches

raspberry yoghurt ice cream

caramel pears with pancakes

quince jelly on scones

basics

roast

tomato

prosciutto + sage sauce

chilli + eggplant

basil soup

tools + tips

pepper grinder

I prefer a wooden grinder with a good adjustable screw for light or coarse grinding. If you purchase a good quality pepper grinder, you'll probably never need to replace it.

deep frying pan

Use a deep frying pan with a heavy base. A frying pan has a larger surface area than a saucepan therefore the liquid evaporates quickly, making the sauce thicker and more flavoursome, faster. If you only have a saucepan, you may need to simmer the sauce for longer than the recipe states.

measuring jugs

These are as important for measuring liquids as cups are for solids. Glass ones are good as you can also use them to ladle large amounts of liquid such as hot stock into risotto. Purchase jugs which have measurements that are easy to read.

ripe cooking tomatoes

Purchase ripe or overripe tomatoes for cooking as they are sweeter and have more flavour. It is best to remove the skins before making the sauce, either by blanching the tomatoes in boiling water or peeling them with a sharp vegetable peeler. You may find that in the cooler months when tomatoes are not at their best, it is better to use canned tomatoes.

tips for success

• Depending on the time of year and what tomatoes are available, your sauce may be a little sharp or acid. This can be easily solved with a pinch or two of sugar • The basic sauce will have a thinner texture and sweeter taste if fresh tomatoes are used, whereas the canned tomatoes will result in a thicker sauce • Use tomato sauce to poach chicken or fish, as a sauce for vegetables or in lasagne, on pizza bases, or as a simple meal over hot pasta topped with grated parmesan cheese and cracked black pepper • When cooking the onions and garlic, don't let them brown as it will taint the delicate flavour of the sauce • When cooking with wine, be aware that poor-tasting wine will show through in the end product. This doesn't mean the vintage reds need to be opened, rather purchase an inexpensive bottle of reasonable quality • After cooking the tomato sauce, don't store or refrigerate it in the saucepan as the acid in the tomatoes may react with the metal in the saucepan • Some people believe that cooked tomato seeds taste bitter and remove all seeds from the tomatoes before cooking. They don't bother me personally, although I only cook tomato sauces using fresh tomatoes when they are well in season and are sweet and juicy.

canned tomatoes

Experiment with the brands available. Italian canned tomatoes are generally good. Look for the ones that are full of whole tomatoes in a thick juice. Avoid cans of chopped tomatoes as they are often a little slushy.

wooden spoons

You can never have enough wooden spoons. Keep them separate for sweet and savoury cooking. If the wooden spoon becomes tainted, put it through the dishwasher or soak for a few hours in a solution of vinegar and water. I like to keep a variety of sizes, too.

canned tomatoes

wooden spoons

deep frying pan

measuring jug   ripe cooking tomatoes   pepper grinder

classic tomato sauce

12 tomatoes or 4 x 440g (14 oz) cans peeled tomatoes, lightly crushed
1 tablespoon oil
1 clove garlic, crushed
2 small onions, chopped
1 cup (8 fl oz) red wine
2 tablespoons chopped oregano, basil or marjoram leaves
cracked black pepper and sea salt

STEP 1 If using fresh tomatoes, place them in a saucepan of boiling water and cook for 1 minute. Drain, peel the skins and chop the tomatoes, reserving any liquid. If using canned tomatoes, there is no need to follow this step.

STEP 2 Heat the oil in a deep frying pan over medium to high heat. Add the garlic and onion and cook for 4 minutes or until soft.

STEP 3 Add the tomato, wine, herbs, pepper and salt and bring to the boil.

STEP 4 Allow the sauce to simmer for 20 minutes if using canned tomatoes and 35 minutes if using fresh tomatoes.

Refrigerate the sauce for up to 3 days. If you are not using the sauce within this time, then freeze the sauce in portion sizes ready to thaw and use. Tomato sauce can be frozen for 4–5 months.

ROAST TOMATO SAUCE Use only fresh tomatoes for this recipe, halve them and place on an oiled baking tray with the cut sides up. Bake in a preheated 180°C (350°F) oven for 30 minutes or until soft. Follow the classic sauce recipe, adding the roast tomatoes instead of the fresh or canned.

PROSCIUTTO AND SAGE TOMATO SAUCE Follow the basic recipe as for the classic tomato sauce. After cooking the onion, add 6 slices of roughly chopped prosciutto to the pan with 2 tablespoons of chopped sage leaves. Serve with extra grilled crisp prosciutto pieces.

TOMATO BASIL SOUP Follow classic tomato sauce recipe and add 2 cups (16 fl oz) of vegetable stock when adding the tomato to the pan. When this has simmered, stir through 1/3 cup of basil (instead of the 2 tablespoons) and serve in deep bowls topped with pepper and parmesan cheese.

CHILLI AND EGGPLANT TOMATO SAUCE Add 2–3 sliced and seeded red chillies to the pan when cooking the garlic and onion. Chop 1 medium-sized, young eggplant (aubergine) into large pieces and add with the tomato, following the classic tomato sauce recipe.

beef

chicken

stock

vegetable veal

fish

tools + tips

strainer

Use a fine strainer to remove cooking particles and small ingredients such as peppercorns from the stock. It is more practical to have a strainer that hooks or rests firmly onto a pot or large bowl for easy straining.

skimming spoon or ladle

Use a large metal spoon to skim the surface of the stock and remove the cooking impurities that cloud its colour. You need to skim the stock, especially meat stocks, every 10–15 minutes when you first begin simmering it. Skimming frequently removes the fat and impurities that rise to the surface and stops them from bubbling back into the stock.

stockpot

A big stockpot or saucepan is essential for making stock. Stockpots vary in price, according to quality and size. If you only want to use the pot for stock, then a cheaper one will suffice. If you want to make other things in it, such as a big pot of shanks, you may find that the base of the pot is not very thick and that the contents will catch on the bottom of the pan. Therefore purchase a multi-purpose stockpot with a substantially heavy base.

seasonings

Herbs such as rosemary, thyme, oregano and marjoram are also good for stocks. Use any combination of vegetables and herbs to create a stock. You may wish to tie herbs and peppercorns in muslin bags—often called a bouquet garni—for easy removal from the stock although straining through a sieve will also remove them.

tips for success

• Allow the stock to simmer only, not boil. If it boils, the result will be a fatty and cloudy stock • Because cooking stock takes time, it is best to make large quantities as in the basic recipe so that you can freeze most of it in small portions. Make sure you label and date the stock. Frozen stock can be kept for up to 1 year if the content is fat free • It is sometimes useful to allow the stock to simmer for another 2–3 hours or until it has doubled in strength. You can use it as a more concentrated flavour or the stock can be frozen in a smaller quantity and water can be added later to return it to its original intensity • To remove fat from the top of warm stock, run a piece of absorbent paper over its surface. This soaks up most of the floating surface fat. Chill the stock to allow the fat to solidify on the top and the fat will then lift off easily • When browning meat and vegetables for stock, be sure they are all well browned but not burnt. Adding burnt meat bones or vegetables to a stock will taint the flavour • Add salt towards the end of simmering stock. Adding salt at the beginning of cooking could result in an over-salty flavour once the water has been reduced from the stock.

vegetables

Use vegetables that are of good quality for a quality stock. Old vegetables will not give the same flavour as fresh ones. If you wish to use vegetables not in their prime then you will need to use more of them to create a well-flavoured stock. Vegetables such as leeks, mushrooms, parsnips, swedes and tomatoes are great to use in stocks.

muslin

Line a strainer or colander with fine muslin or cheesecloth to filter and clarify the stock. If you don't have muslin then use a fine strainer. Muslin is available from good cook shops and from fabric shops.

strainer

vegetables

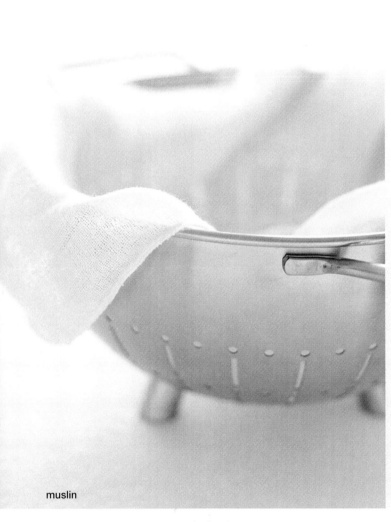

muslin

seasonings

stockpot

skimming spoon

chicken stock

3kg (6 lb) chicken bones
10 litres (320 fl oz) water
1½ cups (12 fl oz) dry white wine
1 onion, chopped
1 carrot, chopped
1 stick celery, chopped
8 black peppercorns
4 stalks parsley
2 bay leaves

STEP 1 Place chicken bones in a large stockpot or saucepan with the water. Bring to a rapid simmer over medium heat.

STEP 2 Add the wine, onion, carrot, celery, peppercorns, parsley and bay leaves and allow to slowly but constantly simmer.

STEP 3 Skim the surface of the stock with a spoon occasionally while it is cooking so that the stock remains clear.

STEP 4 Simmer the stock for 3 hours or until it is well flavoured. Strain the stock through a fine or muslin-lined sieve, cool, and remove any solidified fat from the surface. Makes 5–6 litres.

To keep freshly made stock, cover and refrigerate for 2–3 days. After this time, the stock will need to be reboiled and it will then keep for up to 2 more days after this. Stock can also be frozen in small portions that are easy to thaw and use.

VEGETABLE STOCK Omit the chicken bones. Add to the basic recipe 2 chopped leeks and 1 cup sliced mushrooms. Follow the chicken stock recipe to finish. For a richer or darker vegetable stock, brown the lightly oiled vegetables in a preheated 200°C (400°F) oven for 30 minutes first.

VEAL STOCK Place 3kg (6 lb) of chopped veal bones in a baking dish and brush them with oil. Bake the bones in a preheated 200°C (400°F) oven for 30 minutes and then add the vegetables and bake for a further 30 minutes. Follow the chicken stock recipe, replacing the white wine with red wine.

BEEF STOCK Place 3kg (6 lb) of chopped beef bones in a baking dish and brush them with oil. Bake the bones in a preheated 200°C (400°F) oven for 30 minutes then add the vegetables and bake for a further 30 minutes. Follow the chicken stock recipe, replacing the white wine with red wine.

FISH STOCK Use the heads and bones of three small non-oily fish such as snapper. Follow the chicken stock recipe, adding all other ingredients. Simmer for 20 minutes only or the stock will be sour and then strain through muslin or a very fine strainer.

tempura

batter

pancakes crepes

beer

tools + tips

bowl

Use a dry bowl with high sides so that the batter stays in the bowl when whisking. You may wish to place your bowl on a damp tea towel or kitchen cloth so that it doesn't move around on the bench while you are whisking.

drainer

Metal drainers are ideal for fishing food out of hot oil and for draining it before placing on absorbent kitchen paper. Choose traditional slotted spoon types, or try the bamboo and gold wire ones in a variety of shapes and sizes that are available in Asian supermarkets and good cook shops.

whisk

A wire balloon whisk is best. These come in varying sizes so you may wish to have a small and large one. Whisks are great for everything from smoothing out sauces to beating egg whites the slow way. They are a quick and easy way to remove lumps and incorporate air.

sifter

Use a sifter to remove any lumps from the flour. This will help to create a smooth batter when whisking in the liquid. Sifters come with a winding handle or a squeeze handle for ease of sifting. For convenience, a sieve and a spoon can also be used.

crepe pan

Great for making crepes, these medium-sized pans have gently sloping sides and are the perfect size. Crepe pans may be nonstick, so they don't need greasing. If you don't have a crepe pan, a small shallow frying pan will do a very adequate job.

metal spatula

A spatula or slide makes for easy turning of pancakes and crepes or, if you're game, try your hand at flipping the batter with just the frying pan. I prefer the ones with the wooden handles, although the wider spatulas only seem to have metal handles.

tips for success

• Cook pancake batter after whisking it together, otherwise the rising agents will activate while the batter is in the bowl, leaving your pancakes not the fluffy light creations you were hoping for • Make sure you dry the foods to be dipped in batter so that the batter sticks well. If using a wet food, such as fish, you may wish to coat it lightly in flour first • The oil temperature is very important when deep frying. It should be 190°C (375°F) to ensure that the food seals and is crisp and not soggy with oil • Keep the cooked batter foods or pancake stacks warm by placing them in a warm oven. Cover pancakes and crepes with a clean tea towel to prevent them from drying out • There is no need to leave batter to rest before using it. If you do leave batter for some time before using, you may find that it has thickened and needs extra liquid to thin it to a useable consistency • Drain battered and fried foods on absorbent kitchen paper before serving to remove any excess surface grease.

cooking thermometer

For a crisp deep-fried batter, make sure that your oil reaches the correct temperature (190°C or 375°F). You may wish to use a cooking thermometer that clips onto the side of your saucepan. These thermometers are also useful for making sugar syrups, jams, toffee and caramel.

metal spatulas

bowl and whisks

drainers

sifter

cooking thermometer

crepe pan

batter

2 cups plain (all-purpose) flour
sea salt
1 egg
1½ cups (12 fl oz) milk

STEP 1 Sift the flour and salt into a bowl and make a well in the centre.

STEP 2 Place the egg in a small bowl and beat the egg lightly.

STEP 3 Add the egg and milk to the well in the flour and whisk until the batter is smooth. Add extra milk as necessary to create the desired consistency of the batter.

STEP 4 Use the batter to coat foods like fish and vegetables, and deep fry in hot oil until brown and crisp.

On standing, batter will thicken slightly—add more water or milk to return the batter to its original consistency. Batter without raising agents will keep covered in the refrigerator for up to 2 days. Batter with raising agents should be used soon after making, otherwise the raising agents will deactivate and the pancakes will not be light and fluffy.

PANCAKE BATTER Add an extra egg to batter mixture, 75g (2½ oz) of melted butter, 3 teaspoons baking powder and ⅓ cup of sugar. Add remaining ingredients following recipe for basic mix. Cook over medium heat in a nonstick frying pan until bubbles surface, flip and cook until golden.

BEER BATTER Replace the milk with 1½ cups (12 fl oz) of cold beer and mix the batter until smooth. Use this batter for fish and fish fillets to make the classic beer-battered fish and chips. Use a premium beer with a good malty hops taste to ensure a well-flavoured batter.

CREPE BATTER Add 75g (2½ oz) of melted butter and one extra cup (8 fl oz) of milk to the plain batter, to obtain the consistency of cream. Swirl a little batter in a small, greased crepe pan or frying pan and cook over medium heat until each side is lightly golden. Serve with lemon and sugar.

TEMPURA BATTER Replace the plain flour with 2 cups of fine white rice flour and replace the milk with 1½ cups (12 fl oz) of iced water and mix to a thin consistency. Use this batter to coat vegetables, prawns, fish and chicken strips. Serve with a ready-made dipping sauce.

shortcrust

pastry

sweet

parmesan nut

pepper + mustard

tools + tips

food processor

This is the faster option for making pastry but if you don't have one then use cool fingertips in a rubbing motion to rub the butter through the flour. Use only the pulse button on the food processor for short bursts, making sure you don't over process the flour and butter.

baking weights

You will need either baking weights, uncooked rice or dried beans to blind bake the pastry. Baking weights are small rounds of porcelain or metal and are reusable. Simply cool them after use then store in a sealable container. You can also keep a container of dried beans or rice for this same purpose, to be reused many times. Baking weights keep the pastry from bubbling when baked, therefore creating a thin, even crust.

tart tins

These are available in a huge variety of shapes and sizes. Tart tins with loose bottom trays in them are the easiest to handle. You can also buy large metal rings that sit straight onto any baking tray to make a tart tin. After using, wipe clean and store. Scrubbing with detergents often scratches the surface and can cause the tins to rust.

pastry brush

Great for brushing the top of pies or tart shells or for glazing the tops of tarts, these are available in many different sizes with synthetic or natural bristles.

pastry cutters

If you're going to use pastry cutters to make small tarts, make sure they're sharp and use them with one downward motion to give the pastry a clean edge.

rolling pins

These come in many different shapes and sizes, with or without handles. Use one that feels comfortable to you and apply even pressure with both hands for smooth and even rolling.

flour dredge

Useful for sprinkling a small and even amount of flour onto the work surface before rolling out dough. If the dough is a little sticky, use the flour dredge to lightly sprinkle a little flour over it to prevent it from sticking to the rolling pin. They're not essential although I do like them.

tips for success

• When combining the flour and butter in a food processor, use the pulse button and only process until large crumbs appear and then start adding the iced water • Make sure the butter is hard and cold. Chop it into small pieces before using • It's not necessary to knead the dough for any length of time. A quick knead so that the pastry is a smooth ball is fine • Before rolling, cover the bench with a light sprinkle of flour to ensure the pastry doesn't stick to the surface • Do not stretch the pastry into the tins. Fold the pastry over the rolling pin to lift it from the bench and then unroll it over the tart tin. Ease the pastry into the tin and this will prevent some shrinkage • It is important to rest the pastry in the fridge after making it to keep the butter content cold and also prevent the pastry from shrinking when it is baked. Cover the pastry with plastic wrap so that it doesn't dry out • Blind baking ensures the pastry stays crisp when used with a filling that contains moisture such as a custard or other wet fillings. If you're not using the blind-baked pastry shells the same day you bake them, store in an airtight container to keep them crisp • When a blind-baked tart shell will be used with a moist filling, such as a sweet custard, keep the pastry from becoming soggy by simply brushing the warm pastry shell with a little egg white to seal it from the moisture.

pastry cutters

tart tins

pastry brushes

flour dredge

rolling pins

baking weights

shortcrust pastry

1
2
3
4

2 cups plain (all-purpose) flour
125g (4 oz) cold butter, chopped
iced water

STEP 1 Place the flour and butter into a food processor and process until the mixture has formed rough crumbs. (Do not over process as the dough will become too sticky.)

STEP 2 While motor is running, add enough iced water to form a soft dough. Remove from the food processor and knead lightly. Wrap in plastic wrap and refrigerate for 30 minutes before rolling to prevent the pastry from shrinking when baked.

STEP 3 Roll out pastry on a lightly floured surface or on a sheet of nonstick baking paper until 2–3mm (⅛ inch) thick. Line the desired tin or tins with pastry, easing it into the shell without stretching it. Chill pastry in tin for 5 minutes.

STEP 4 Blind bake the pastry by pricking the base and the sides of the pastry with a fork. Cover with a sheet of nonstick baking paper and fill the tin with baking weights or dried beans or rice. Bake the pastry case in a preheated 190°C (375°F) oven for 5 minutes. Remove weights and paper, and return pastry to the oven for a further 5 minutes or until it is light gold in colour.

If using the pastry within 3 days, store the cooked shell in an airtight container. To keep the pastry shell for longer, wrap in plastic wrap and freeze for up to 3 months. Thaw and re-crisp the pastry in a 180°C (350°F) oven for 3–5 minutes before using. You may also freeze the uncooked pastry shell in the tin for up to 3 months. To use, thaw the pastry and follow the blind-baking instructions as above.

SWEET SHORTCRUST PASTRY The simplest variation of the lot. Just add 3 tablespoons of caster (superfine) sugar to the flour before processing. This is your stock standard pastry for any sweet tart or pie and can be filled with anything from lemon curd to rich chocolate ganache.

NUT SHORTCRUST Add ⅓ cup of ground nuts such as almonds, hazelnuts or walnuts to flour before processing. For a sweet version, add 2 tablespoons of caster (superfine) sugar also. Try savoury fillings with rich cheeses. The sweet version can be filled with just about anything.

PARMESAN SHORTCRUST PASTRY Add $1/3$ cup of shredded parmesan cheese to flour before processing. Use this pastry for savoury tarts or pies, such as a tart spread with fresh goats curd or ricotta and topped with roast tomatoes and sliced olives or pesto.

PEPPER AND MUSTARD SHORTCRUST Add 1 teaspoon of cracked black pepper and 2 tablespoons of seeded mustard before processing the flour. Use this pastry for savoury fillings of vegetables and cheeses or for adding a kick to a standard recipe such as an egg and bacon pie.

olive

dough

muscatel + cinnamon

pizza

calzone

tools + tips

dough hook

If you have a set of beaters on a stand that came with your electric mixer, check if it includes a dough hook attachment. It may be a consideration when purchasing your next mixer as the attachment does take most of the hard work out of making dough. A single dough hook is more effective than an electric mixer that comes with two beaters. You can use the dough hook to make the dough and then knead it, reducing time and muscle action.

rolling pins

These come in a variety of shapes, sizes and materials such as wood, plastic, marble and steel. Choose one according to your frequency of use and make sure that you feel comfortable using it to roll an even dough. There is no need to wash wooden rolling pins, simply wipe clean and remove any sticky dough using a pastry scraper or blunt knife.

seeds

Seeds can be kneaded into the dough, before baking, for flavour or sprinkled over a dough that has been brushed with oil, water or egg. Seeds to try include sesame, linseed, poppy, sunflower and pumpkin.

flour

You can use many different flours to create a base dough. Flours such as soya, rye, wholemeal and chick pea can be used. With heavier flours such as rye, soya and chick pea, you may wish to use half plain (all-purpose) flour and half of the heavier flour so the dough is not too dense.

tips for success

• When adding the water to the yeast mixture, make sure that it is lukewarm. If the temperature is hotter, it may kill or deactivate the yeast • Yeast is a living organism that needs sugar, its form of food, to activate but too much sugar will also kill the yeast, as will salt • When kneading, fold the front of the dough to the middle, press it into the centre and then press forward with your hand. Use the other hand to give the dough a quarter turn and repeat the process until the dough is smooth and elastic • The dough is kneaded sufficiently when it feels smooth and elastic. If you press it with your thumb, it should bounce back • When yeast is rising, keep it covered, away from draughts and warm, but don't let it get too hot either or the yeast will die. The optimum temperature for yeast to grow is 27°C (80°F) • Cool the cooked bread on wire racks to ensure it has a crisp crust • The dough needs to be kneaded sufficiently so that the gluten strands in the flour are developed and elastic. Then when the yeast gives off its carbon dioxide, raising and aerating, the dough will stretch and hold like a framework • Add sugar, fruits, vegetables and other flavourings after the first rising of the dough to avoid destroying the yeast.

muscles

Make sure yours are in good working order if you don't have an electric mixer with a dough hook or just for the normal kneading and rolling that making dough requires.

yeast

I prefer dry yeast for convenience, but make sure it hasn't run past its expiry date as then it may not activate. The first step in the basic dough recipe is a good test to ensure the yeast is alive as the bubbles on the surface of the mixture signal activity. Yeast needs warmth, sugar and moisture to grow. Too much heat, sugar, salt or fat may kill the yeast. Yeast works by releasing tiny bubbles of carbon dioxide therefore making the dough stretch and rise.

rolling pin

seeds

dough hook

yeast

tins

flours

dough

1 teaspoon active dry yeast
pinch sugar
2/3 cup (5½ fl oz) lukewarm water
2 cups plain (all-purpose) flour
½ teaspoon sea salt
¼ cup (2 fl oz) olive oil

STEP 1 Place the yeast, sugar and water in a bowl and mix to combine.
Stand the mixture in a warm place until it has bubbles on the surface.

STEP 2 Place the flour, salt, oil and yeast mixture into the bowl of an electric mixer
fitted with a dough hook and mix well until a smooth dough forms.

STEP 3 Knead the dough with the dough hook for 5 minutes or by hand on a
lightly floured surface for 25 minutes or until it is smooth and elastic.

STEP 4 Place the dough in a clean, oiled bowl, cover with a damp clean tea towel,
and allow to stand in a warm place for 20 minutes or until it has doubled
in size. Knead the dough lightly before shaping and placing in a tin. Cover
and stand until doubled in size. Bake in a preheated 200°C (400°F) oven
for 25 minutes or until golden and hollow sounding when tapped.

If you are not using the dough after the proving stage, wrap it tightly in plastic wrap
and place it in the freezer to arrest the growth of the yeast. Before shaping and
baking, allow the dough to thaw and knead it lightly. Always allow the dough to
prove a second time before baking. Dough to be baked in a loaf can be shaped
and frozen in the tin—simply thaw the dough and allow it to prove before baking.
If adding flavourings to the dough, add them after the dough has defrosted, before
the second proving. Dough will freeze for up to 3 months.

CALZONE Divide risen dough into 4 portions. Roll them on a floured surface until 1cm (½ inch) thick. Place fillings such as cheeses, grilled vegetables or meats, pesto etc, on half of the dough. Fold over dough to enclose filling. Bake in a preheated 200°C (400°F) oven for 25 minutes or until golden.

PIZZA BASES Divide the risen dough into 4 equal portions and roll on a lightly floured surface until the dough is the desired thickness. Add toppings and bake in a 200°C (400°F) oven for 15–20 minutes or until the base is golden and the topping cooked.

OLIVE BREAD Roll risen dough on a floured surface until 2cm (¾ inch) thick. Place on a baking tray. Press in a few olives and rosemary sprigs. Sprinkle with salt and olive oil. Cover with a damp tea towel; stand until doubled in size. Bake in a preheated 200°C (400°F) oven for 20 minutes.

MUSCATEL + CINNAMON BREAD Knead 1 cup seedless muscatels, 2 tablespoons sugar and 2 teaspoons ground cinnamon into dough. Place dough in a small loaf tin. Cover with a damp tea towel and stand until doubled in size. Bake in a preheated 200°C (400°F) oven for 35 minutes.

glossary

angel hair pasta
A very thin, tubular pasta—hence its name. Substitutes include spaghetti, linguini and thin fettucine. Avaliable fresh or dry, plain or flavoured.

arborio rice
Taking its name from a village in the Piedmont region of northern Italy, this short-grain rice is used for risotto. It releases some of its starch when cooked, making a creamy savoury rice dish. Other varieties used for risotto include violone and carnaroli.

balmain or moreton bay bugs
Small flat Australian crustaceans with a peculiar body appearance. The sweet and delicate tail meat is similar to a small lobster or crayfish. All of the meat is found in the tail which is easily removed in one piece. They can be purchased green (raw) or cooked.

bamboo steamer
An Asian bamboo container with a lid and a slatted base. Placed on top of a saucepan of boiling water, the steamer holds the food to be steamed. A metal steamer can also be used. Available from Asian food stores and most cook shops.

blanching
A cooking method in which foods are plunged into boiling water for a few seconds, removed and then refreshed under cold water which stops the cooking process. Used to heighten the colour and flavour, to firm flesh and to loosen skins.

bocconcini
Fresh Italian mozzarella balls sold in a water or brine solution. Available from delicatessens and supermarkets. Traditionally made from buffalo milk but more commonly found made from cows milk.

caper berries
The flower of the caper bush becomes an oval berry or fruit which is full of tiny seeds. Caper berries are sold with tender stems attached in vinegar or a brine solution. Available from good delicatessens.

cellophane noodles
Cellophane or beanthread noodles are made from the starch of mung beans and come as vermicelli or as flat, wide noodles. They are difficult to cut and separate when dried, so buy them in small bundles if possible. They need to be soaked in boiling water for 10 minutes or until soft, and then drained. You can also deep fry them straight from the packet.

chervil
A delicate, lacey-looking herb with a faint, sweet aniseed flavour. Its flavour diminishes after being chopped, so add to food just before serving.

chilli oil
Oil infused with the heat and flavour of chillies. It often has a red tinge. Different brands have different strengths so check them for heat by tasting a drop before using. Available from Asian food stores and delicatessens.

chinese barbecue duck
A cooked duck, spiced and barbecued in the traditional Chinese barbecue style. Available from Chinese barbecue shops or from Chinese food stores.

chinese barbecue pork
Cooked pork meat, spiced and barbecued in the traditional Chinese barbecue style. Available from Chinese barbecue shops or from Chinese food stores.

chinese cooking wine
A cooking wine made from rice which is similar to dry sherry. Often labelled as shao hsing in Asian supermarkets.

chinese five spice powder
An equal mixture of the spices cinnamon, anise pepper, star anise clove and fennel. Available from most supermarkets or Asian food stores.

crème fraîche
A mixture of soured cream and fresh cream. Lighter and not as thick as the easily obtainable sour cream although this does make a good substitute.

fish sauce
Clear, amber-tinted liquid that is drained from salted, fermented fish. A very important flavouring in Thai cuisine. Available from supermarkets and Asian cuisine stores.

fresh rice noodles

Fresh rice noodles come in a variety of widths and lengths and are located in the refrigerator section of Asian food stores and some supermarkets. Keep them only for a few days in the refrigerator. To prepare, soak noodles in hot to boiling water for 1 minute, separating them gently with a fork, then drain. Fresh rice noodles also come as rolls which can be steamed as a side dish or filled and steamed.

gravlax

From Nordic origins, a salmon fillet that has been cured in a combination of rock salt, sugar and herbs. It is then sliced thinly and resembles smoked salmon, but has a more delicate flavour. Available in some supermarkets and good delicatessens.

haloumi

Fine white cheese made from sheep's milk. It has a stringy texture and is usually sold in brine. Available from delicatessens and some supermarkets.

harissa

A hot paste of red chillies, garlic, spices and olive oil. Available in tubes or jars from delicatessens.

hoisin sauce

A thick, sweet-tasting Chinese sauce made from fermented soy beans, sugar, salt and red rice. Use as a dipping sauce or glaze. Traditionally used for Peking duck. Available from Asian food stores and supermarkets.

hokkien noodles

Round yellow wheat noodles available from the refrigerator section of supermarkets and Asian food stores. Place noodles in a bowl and cover them with hot to boiling water. Soak for 1–2 minutes or until the noodles have softened, and then drain.

hommus

A paste made from chick peas, tahini, olive oil, garlic and lemon juice, from the Middle Eastern Countries. Use it as a spread or dip.

juniper berry

A dark-coloured mild spiced berry that complements game and red meats. Crush lightly before use to release the flavour. Available as a moist dried berry from good delicatessens and spice shops.

kaffir lime

These fragrant leaves are crushed or shredded and used in cooking and the limes are used for their juice, mainly in Thai cuisine. Available as packets of leaves or as limes from Asian food stores.

laksa paste

The base to an Asian, rich coconut milk soup. A laksa paste can contain ground spices, herbs, ginger, shrimp paste and lemongrass. The soup contains a spiced coconut broth, noodles, vegetables such as bean sprouts, mint and coriander, seafood or chicken. Laksa paste is available from supermarkets or Asian food stores. You may need to try a few to find a good brand.

lemongrass

A tall, lemon-scented grass used in Asian, mainly Thai, cooking. Peel away outer leaves and use the tender root end of the grass. Chop finely or use in pieces to infuse flavour and remove from dish before serving. Available from Asian food stores and good fruit and vegetable shops.

linguini

Long, thin pasta with square cut edges. Similar to flat spaghetti. Substitute spaghetti or fettucine.

marscapone

An Italian, triple-cream, curd-style fresh cheese, which has a similar consistency to double or thick cream. Available from good delicatessens and some supermarkets.

miso

A thick paste made from fermented and processed soy beans. Red miso is a combination of barley and soy beans and white or yellow miso is a combination of rice and soy beans.

muscato d'asti

A fruity sparkling Italian dessert wine generally with flavours of stone fruit and citrus. Low in alcohol content, this is also said to be the perfect breakfast wine.

nori sheets

Dried seaweed pressed into square sheets. Use for nori rolls, soups and Japanese cuisine. Keep dry and store in an airtight container. Available in packets from Asian food stores.

palm sugar

Sap of the palm tree concentrated into a heavy, moist sugar. Sold in block form and should be grated or shaved before using. Used mainly in Thai cooking. I prefer the darker one for its stronger caramel flavour. Substitute brown sugar.

pancetta

Italian rolled and cured meat similar to prosciutto only not as salty or as tough. Can be eaten in thin slices from the roll or cooked in dishes.

pasta

3 cups flour
4 large eggs
2 teaspoons salt

Place flour on a bench top in a mound. Make a hole in the mound and break up the eggs and put salt into the hole. Break up eggs with a fork and gradually add flour to the eggs until a rough dough forms. (You can do this step in a food processor.) Place dough on a lightly floured surface (you may need to add a little flour to make the dough manageable) and knead until it is smooth. Cut pasta into 4 pieces and roll through a pasta machine or using a rolling pin until it is the desired thickness. Cut pasta into shapes or cover with a damp cloth if you are using it a few hours later. Cook pasta in plenty of boiling water until it is al dente. Make sure the water stays boiling while the pasta cooks. To dry, hang pasta over a suspended wooden spoon or a clean broom handle for 1–2 hours, until it's dry and hard. Store pasta in airtight containers.
Makes 1 quantity.

preserved lemon

Originally from the Middle Eastern countries, these are whole lemons preserved in salt and lemon juice. Remove flesh and white pith, using only the preserved rind in cooking.

prosciutto

A type of Italian 'ham' which has been salted and air dried. Sold in paper thin slices for eating raw or for using in cooked dishes.

proving

Process when a yeast mixture or dough is left covered in a warm draught-free place to rise or prove.

quince paste

A thick and fragrant paste made from quinces, sugar and lemon juice. It is often sliced and served with cheese. Available from good delicatessens.

ramekins

Small, ovenproof dishes used for soufflés, crème brûlées, and other individually served foods.

red curry paste

A hot and spicy paste of ground red chillies, herbs and spices. Available in bottles from supermarkets or Asian food stores.

rice paper rounds

Fine transparent circles made from a paste of rice and water. Before using, brush or dip in warm water until they are pliable. Available from Asian food stores.

roma tomatoes

Also known as egg, Italian or plum tomatoes. These oval tomatoes have good flavour making them great for cooking and eating.

sashimi tuna

Finest quality tuna cut in an Asian or Japanese style. It is very tender and is used raw in Japanese cuisine. Often used sparingly due to price. Available from good fish markets.

semi-dried tomatoes

Wedges of ripe tomato that have been semi-sundried so they are still soft and moist. Often sold in flavoured oil. Available from some supermarkets and delicatessens.

shiitake mushrooms

Originally from Japan and Korea, these mushrooms have a distinctive, full-bodied flavour. They have brownish tops with creamy undersides. Available from good fruit and vegetable stores.

star anise

A star-shaped spice with a sweet aniseed flavour. Often used in Asian and Indian cooking. Available also as a powder. Purchase from Asian food stores or spice shops.

thai basil

Includes many varieties such as holy, purple and sweet. Any of these can be used in Thai or Asian cuisine. Substitute any type of basil.

tortillas

Cornbread baked in flat discs used to wrap foods or eaten as bread. Wheat flour tortillas are another popular variety. Traditionally from Mexico and the South American countries. Available in varying sizes from supermarkets.

udon noodles

White Japanese wheat noodles, which can be purchased fresh (from the refrigerator section) or dried. They come in a variety of thicknesses and lengths. Available from Japanese or Asian food stores.

wasabi

A spice that comes from the knobbly root of the Japanese plant *Wasabia japonica*. A traditional condiment served with Japanese sushi and sashimi. It has the same warming or nasal-stinging sensation as horseradish. Available as a paste or powder from Asian food stores.

vanilla beans

Cured pods from the vanilla orchid. Used whole, often split, to infuse flavour into custard or cream-based recipes. Also available is pure vanilla extract, which is a thick, dark, sticky liquid, and makes a good substitute for vanilla beans.

vietnamese mint

Not a member of the mint family although it is called mint. It has long, green narrow leaves with purple markings. It is bitter, zesty and pungent in flavour. Available from Asian food stores.

conversion chart

1 cup = 250 ml (8 fl oz)
1 Australian tablespoon = 20 ml
(4 teaspoons)
1 UK tablespoon = 15 ml
(3 teaspoons)
1 teaspoon = 5ml

CUP CONVERSIONS
1 cup baby English spinach = 60g (2 oz)
1 cup basil leaves, whole, firmly packed = 50g (1¾ oz)
1 cup cheese, parmesan, finely grated = 100g (3¼ oz)
1 cup chick peas = 220g (7 oz)
1 cup coconut cream = 250g (8 oz)
1 cup coconut, dessicated = 90g (3 oz)
1 cup coriander leaves, whole = 30g (1 oz)
1 cup couscous = 200g (6½ oz)
1 cup flour, white = 125g (4 oz)
1 cup lentils = 200g (6½ oz)
1 cup olives, stoned = 155g (5 oz)
1 cup parsley, flat-leaf (Italian), whole = 20g (¾ oz)
1 cup polenta = 150g (5 oz)
1 cup rice, raw = 220g (7 oz)
1 cup rocket (arugula) leaves, roughly chopped = 45g (1½ oz)
1 cup sugar, caster (superfine) = 220g (7 oz)
1 cup sugar, white = 250g (8 oz)

index